Right from the Start

CREATE A SANE, SOFT, WELL-BALANCED HORSE

by

MICHAEL SCHAFFER

Trafalgar Square Publishing
North Pomfret, Vermont

First published in 2001 by
Trafalgar Square Publishing
North Pomfret, Vermont 05053

Printed in Hong Kong

Copyright © 2001 Michael Schaffer

Diagrams © 2001 Michael Schaffer

Disclaimer
The author and publisher shall have neither liability nor responsibility to any person or entity with respect to any loss or damage caused or alleged to be caused directly or indirectly by the information contained in this book. While the book is as accurate as the author can make it, there may be errors, omissions, and inaccuracies.

Library of Congress Cataloging-in-Publication Data
Schaffer, Michael.
　　　　Right from the start / Michael Schaffer.
　　　　　　　p. cm.
　　　　Includes bibliographical reference (p.).
　　　　ISBN 1-57076-208-2
Horses—Training. 2. Horsemanship.　I. Title.
SF287 .S29 2001
798.2'3—dc21　　　　　　　　　　　　　2001033308

Illustration Credits
Photos: Marty Schwind (pages 39, 41, 117, 121, 133–138, 140, 143, 144);
Jean Van Dyke (pages 55, 65, 66, 68, 69, 90); Juanita Petterson (pages 1, 151);
T.C. Meagher (pages 15, 119, 126, 146, 148); Al Hough (pages 56–59, 70, 76, 77, 104, 124); Mike Schaffer (pages 63, 79, 153, 163, 165, 167).
Line Art: Beth Preston (pages 75, 95, 97, 141).
Diagrams: computer generated by Mike Schaffer using TurboCad 2D.

Cover and book design by Carrie Fradkin
Typeface: Rotis Serif

Color separations by Tenon & Polert Colour Scanning Ltd.

10 9 8 7 6 5 4 3 2 1

Table of Contents

Dedication   iv
Acknowledgments   iv
Note to the Reader   v

PART ONE—OF MAN AND BEAST AND SUGAR CUBES   *1*
Chapters 1   Partners   *3*
        2   Training   *7*
        3   Learning   *11*
        4   Five Rules   *17*

PART TWO—ON HORSEBACK IN A PHYSICAL WORLD   *33*
        5   Terms   *35*
        6   The Aids of Reason   *43*
        7   Correctly Speaking . . .   *49*
        8   The Fine Art of Doing Nothing!   *53*
        9   Contact   *61*
       10   Rein Effects   *73*
       11   Reiny Daze   *81*

PART THREE—THAT DELICATE BALANCE!   *87*
       12   Developing Working Gaits   *89*
       13   True Balance   *93*
       14   Direction, Angle, and Bend   *99*
       15   Your Natural Circle   *103*
       16   Your Horse's Natural Circle   *107*

PART FOUR—LITTLE BY LITTLE   *113*
       17   First Touch   *115*
       18   Soften, Bend, and Move Into the Hand   *129*
       19   Under Saddle, and on to the Aids   *161*
       20   Falling In and Out   *169*
       21   Changing Bend and Direction   *175*
       22   Half-Halts   *183*
       23   Transitions   *191*
       24   Conclusion   *197*

Glossary   *199*
Index   *200*

Dedication

This book is dedicated to Mom, Dad, all horses everywhere, and the promise that these are the last clichés you'll find in it.

Acknowledgments

I'd like to thank Alex Konyot for his vast knowledge and his two favorite sayings, "Little by little until he begins to understand," and "The least you do, the better you are." In many ways this book is just my poor attempt to figure out how he was able to accomplish so much with so little effort in so little time while always making it look so easy.

Of course, without Martha Cook, managing editor, and Caroline Robbins, publisher, at Trafalgar Square, this would never have been a book at all. Now, they never once made the suggestion that this project would be easy, effortless, or quick. To the contrary, they were quite clear about how large an undertaking it was, how long it would take, and what mistakes first-time authors are likely to make. Yet, despite this foreknowledge, they still took on a veritable unknown with a pathetically written first draft—presumably just because I had something to say. By the way, I did make every mistake they thought I would—at least once.

No one in the horse world can go it alone, and I've been very fortunate in the friends and supporters I've had along the way—Juanita and her group at Justamere Farm, Squeek and her gang at Nature's Last Stand, Drs. Malcolm and Rhoda Marks, the folks on the horse forum, cousin Helene, and my old friend Cathy who once loaned her trailer to a total stranger, and started many ripples on their way across the pond.

Note to the Reader

In this book, I make some assumptions about you. I assume you are not a rank beginner, and may well have been riding for years. The rider exercises and riding techniques included in this book are intended to help you get the most out of the training program this book proposes—not to teach you to ride.

I also assume you have had exposure to many descriptions and words commonly used in the riding community that are confusing because of the actual and apparent conflicts within and between them. For this reason, I occasionally begin a discussion of what a word or phrase means, by first stating what it does not mean, and why other explanations of it are faulty. If, in fact, you have not heard the other descriptions, you may wonder why I am off on a particular tirade, but if you can persevere for just a few paragraphs, I do get on to the business of explaining the word or phrase in question very early on.

Finally, I would like to make it very clear that I do not assume you are a rider of any particular discipline or style. This is not a book about jumping, eventing, reining, dressage, endurance, or just plain riding on the trails. Rather, this book is intended to help you help your horse to do any or all of the above more comfortably and happily. However, I am who I am, and I have occasionally referred to the movements performed in classical riding. For those not familiar with these, I've included a very brief description of them at the back of the book.

PART ONE
Of Man and Beast and Sugar Cubes

1

Partners

*I*t always comes down to basics. If things are going well, it's because your horse's basics are good. If things aren't going so well, invariably there's a problem with them. It makes no difference if you're starting a brand new baby or trying to improve your mount of many years, it always comes down to the quality of this, your horse's most important training.

But everybody says that. And everybody says exactly what good basics look like. But very few tell you how to get them. Most just tell you good basics are important, assume your horse has them, and proceed to the next step.

It's true that some gifted horses seem to come by good basics naturally. It's also true that some gifted children learn to read before entering school. But can you imagine a school system that assumes all students could teach themselves to read?

A fact is that many books on dressage assume horses can begin—already balanced and moving freely forward on a 20-meter circle. They can't. Books on jumping assume that if ridden over enough cavaletti and grids, horses learn to engage before a fence and jump with rounded backs. They don't. Trail riders assume horses are "rider wise" as soon as they stop bucking, and need only experience to become "trail wise." They're not.

These assumptions have left gaping holes in our horse's training. We have taught horses they *should* be ridden—that they *should* let us sit on their backs and point them where we want to go. But we haven't shown them *how* to be ridden—*how* to carry us in a balanced gait, and do a correct transition. The difference between teaching a horse he *should* be ridden, and showing him *how* to be ridden is not just an esoteric fine point. It's HUGE! It affects everything—from how well you do at your next show, to the very core of the relationship with your horse.

Your horse is not resistant and evasive— if he was, you couldn't ride him.

Today we only ride for the relationship—for the sheer joy of it. We don't need to ride for any reason—we just need to ride. We need the little time we get to spend with our horses to be time well spent with our best friends. We need a partnership with them.

But, a horse that doesn't know *how* to be ridden, can't be a partner. He can only muddle through to the best of his limited ability. When he fails we are left with the original assumption—that he *can* do it, and from that we create the second assumption, that he must be "resistant" or "evasive" if he doesn't.

Poor basics will always lead to these words. "Resistance" and "evasion" have so permeated the world of riding they are now a culture unto themselves. They turn our best friend and partner into our adversary. They give us permission to blame the horse instead of looking for the flaw in the method. They allow us to believe we can solve problems with tighter nosebands, stronger bits, or the latest device on the market, instead of forcing us to think we may not be training correctly. These words are so enticing—so effortless—they're addictive. They're used a million times a day with no more thought or reason than the chain smoker uses when lighting up another cigarette.

When the words finally fail, as they must, and the frustration turns to anger and then fear, as it so often does, they are replaced with, "Maybe you need another horse." The cycle is complete—the relationship is totally destroyed, and your best friend and partner is now a commodity on the market.

It doesn't have to be this way. Your horse is not resistant and evasive—if he was, you couldn't ride him. I say this from the experience of having seen what happens when horses have had enough of our assumptions and see us as that "damned human race." They refuse to be ridden at all. If you think your horse is resistant and evasive, he's probably as confused and frustrated as you. He's certainly out of balance, which makes him a little clumsy, stiff and uncomfortable. But, he's not resistant and he's not evasive. He needs to learn *how* to be ridden. He needs you to explain it to him.

Trying to ride a horse without good basics is terribly difficult, but teaching proper basics is easy. Trying to train a horse without basics takes forever, but schooling (or re-schooling) basics, can take as little as a few months. Most people see fairly dramatic results in just a few days, and some, in just a few hours. The age and experience of your horse is no barrier. The training techniques and methods I present in this book work on green babies that have never been ridden, and, by giving them a fresh beginning, on horses that have been carrying riders the wrong way for years.

Trying to ride a horse without good basics is terribly difficult, but teaching him proper basics is easy.

2 Training

The entire process of training can be reduced to one sentence, "First ask correctly, then make correct, then reward." This sentence describes the *exercise-reward cycle*. The exercise-reward cycle is the means by which training is accomplished.

Although this is a book about training horses, my favorite example of the exercise-reward cycle is teaching a dog to sit. First the request is made, then the dog is encouraged to sit, and finally, the dog is rewarded when he does. In this example, the trainer "first asks correctly" by telling the dog to "sit." The trainer then "makes correct" by lifting the dog's head to encourage him to give the correct response and sit. When the dog does sit, he is "then rewarded." The next time through the exercise-reward cycle, the steps are followed more or less in the same fashion. Usually, after several repetitions, the dog will anticipate the lift of its head, and sit on his own accord. When the dog does sit in response to just the verbal request and is rewarded even more generously, he will begin to understand the action associated with the spoken word "sit."

We have, by this means, defined the word *sit* to the dog. We have connected his action of sitting to an audible sound. He now comprehends an English word. With the same method used to define an individual word to the puppy, we can define individual *aids* to the horse. Then, using these individual aids, we can build phrases and sentences that allow our horses to understand even the most complex requests. Yes, training a horse is more intricate than teaching a puppy to sit, but the basic principles remain the same. So, to further examine the exercise-reward cycle, let's return to the above example for a few moments.

The spoken word sit can be equated to our giving an *aid*. Aids, which request, encourage and allow, are discussed in detail in Chapter 6, *The Aids of Reason*. Lifting the dog's head is a correction, which is clear effective and over with. Corrections are discussed in Chapter 7, *Correctly Speaking*. Reward may differ, depending upon the circumstances, but it is always extremely important.

First ask correctly,

then make correct,

then reward.

The request itself, the word *sit* when training a dog, should be clear and isolated. To make the verbal request clear and isolated, there should be at least a moment before and after it is spoken when there is silence. A direct correlation exists between this example and our riding. For instance, when teaching a specific response to a particular rein aid, the hand must be soft and quiet before the aid is applied and then again afterward. In this way the horse can associate the particular action with the specific request. The same is true for teaching the correct responses to the seat and leg.

The aid or request is defined with a correction (lifting the dog's head in the above example). The correction must come soon enough to be related to the request. It is difficult to say precisely how much time, but it should be long enough for the subject to have had a chance to hear, feel, and react to the request, while not so long that he loses the association with it. Corrections must have the desired effect. If the trainer is going to lift the puppy's head, it must be done so the dog does sit down—anything less just leads to confusion and resentment. Yet, while being effective it must not be frightening or painful. The object is to teach the dog to sit, not to fear us. The same concept applies to training a horse.

The purpose of reward is to convey that a specific requested action has been accomplished. It should also be used to make sure that total relaxation is restored. In the case of teaching a physically stressful exercise to a horse, the reward should be long enough so that he is completely rested and ready to continue before anything else is requested of him.

Throughout all training, the exercise-reward cycle is the only positive teaching method available. The tasks requested and the techniques for defining the aids vary tremendously, but the underlying process remains the same. For that reason, at the onset of training, whether teaching a puppy to sit or a young horse to go, stop, or bend, the exercise-reward cycle itself will be part of the lesson. In other words, the youngster will not only be learning a specific task, but learning to learn as well.

Throughout all training, the exercise-reward cycle is the only positive teaching method available.

3 Learning

The exercise-reward cycle describes how we present information but does not explain how a horse accepts it. Years of observation have led me to believe the learning process is more complex and interesting than the teaching process.

At first it may not be clear to the horse why he is being rewarded at the end of the exercise-reward cycle. To illustrate, let's use the example of teaching a horse to stand quietly while nothing at all is happening. The teaching task is to have the horse stand quietly while the handler walks to, from, and around him (specific techniques for this exercise are discussed in the Chapter 17, *First Touch*).

Standing next to the horse, a handler says the word "stand" as he steps back. Since he stood quietly, the horse is approached and patted, "Good boy." Again the word "stand" is repeated as a step back is taken. Once again the horse stands quietly, is approached and rewarded. On the third repetition of the exercise-reward cycle, the command is repeated as another step back is taken, only this time, the horse takes a step toward the handler. What is the problem here? The horse was just shown that if he stood still he would be rewarded. How could he find that confusing?

In truth, it may never be known exactly what the horse was thinking with regard to the exercise or if he was thinking of it at all. However, to proceed in a rational way, it is necessary to have some theory about his thought process. Empirical evidence makes it appear that during early repetitions of the exercise-reward cycle, the horse is "guessing." In other words, whenever a horse is presented with a new request from the rider, he's simply going to take a guess at what it is the rider wants and then act upon it. If the action fails to earn a reward, he will guess again and take a new action based upon that. Further, once he is rewarded, he will remember many of the incorrect guesses he made and actions he took, but he will not know which particular action or combination of actions actually led to the reward.

The horse's attempts to figure out what we want are all too often called resistance and evasion.

However, on each repetition of the exercise-reward cycle, the horse will make the right guess more rapidly because he is using what he learned in the preceding cycle. Based on his previous experience, he begins to eliminate actions that did not earn reward before. In addition, he spends less time acting on guesses that previously proved incorrect—as though once he has begun an action, he remembers that it didn't work before, so he abandons it and tries something else. Once you've seen enough horses react in essentially the same way to the same lessons, it becomes plain that our horses are considering their situation and using a process of trial and error to methodically eliminate invalid guesses and actions. Unfortunately, these attempts to figure out what we want are all too often called resistance and evasions.

We can be fairly certain that our horses are going through this process because if they were not, the horse would on the second and each successive attempt immediately do the right thing. While this happens, it does not happen frequently, and almost never with unschooled, or poorly schooled horses.

Over the long term, by consistently teaching lessons in this manner, the horse realizes that what we want is near the end of the list of things he did. As a result, the process of figuring out what we want becomes much shorter. The horse is learning to learn. He is beginning to understand the exercise-reward cycle.

If you think I'm giving horses too much credit for being able to maintain a list of behaviors in memory and then logically proceed to eliminate incorrect ones, think of how many times experienced riders have warned others against schooling a dressage test from start to finish. They worry the horse will begin to anticipate the next movement. Implicit in that remark is the belief that a horse will memorize an entire test and deduce that since he has just done A, B, and C, he is going to be asked to perform D next. I never held much stock in that notion until I accidentally taught a horse of mine that if he did the second half of the Prix St. George test he was done for the day. Think about that. Some people cannot memorize a Training Level test and here my horse took it upon himself to memorize a much more complex series of movements.

The horse's excellent memory, as well as his reactions to new ideas, supports the theory mentioned earlier that he is going through a methodical process of trial and error trying to figure out what is being asked for. This is especially apparent when training from the ground where all of his reactions can be seen. A good example is teaching a horse to move away from the whip. Typically, when learning this exercise a horse will first kick out at the whip, and then he might take a step back or try to walk through the hand—all incorrect actions. Finally, he will just pick up the leg in question and move it alone, forward and under himself. As that is the correct response, the trainer rewards him. In the next repetition of the exercise, one of the incorrect responses will normally be gone; for instance, he may not try to take that backward step. By the fourth or fifth repetition, the horse begins to lift his leg as though to kick and then, in mid-motion, stops and puts his foot forward and under himself. Teach several horses this exercise from the ground and their reactions are so consistent and predictable that the inevitable conclusion is that horses learn in a logical, progressive manner.

Because horses learn in this logical, progressive manner, they must be taught in a logical, progressive manner. For example, it would be rare for a young horse with no experience or previous jump schooling to willingly go over a three-foot fence. However, if you begin teaching him to jump by taking him over a rail lying on the ground and then gradually raise the rail, it is the rare horse that will not happily jump a three-foot fence after a little while.

The way horses learn and the ways we have to present information are constant throughout the training process. Jumping is an obvious case—but a subtle, unsung example is in teaching a horse to relax his muscles and bend. Asking for an even bend throughout the horse's body is the equivalent of the three-foot fence—we have to begin with easier exercises and work up to it.

Even more fascinating than the way horses learn initially is the evidence that suggests a second stage of learning. It appears that horses are not satisfied with just knowing what it is we want, they want to know about it as

Because horses learn in this logical, progressive manner, they must be taught in a logical, progressive manner.

well. This is also completely in keeping with our understanding of their nature and observations of their behavior.

Horses, like people, have a playful nature (fig. 1). People play with new toys (read into that, new cars, skis, or computers). After a while, they may use the new toys, but they do not play with them much. The most universal example is the new car. No one ever picks a new car up from the dealer in the afternoon, takes it home and parks it in the driveway until it is time to "use" the car the next morning to go to work. The evening of the new car's arrival is spent testing it out or cruising around. The car is being played with. It is also being studied. Although the proud owner knows how to drive, by trying out the new car, he is learning about its peculiarities and getting a feel for it.

It appears that horses are not satisfied with just knowing what it is we want, they want to know all about it as well.

A more rudimentary example is of a young child or a horse picking up a dead branch, swinging it for a few seconds, and throwing it away. Both are learning the same things, for the same reasons, in exactly the same manner.

Horses need some time to "play" with the new things we teach them too. Experience shows that while a horse is learning something new, he will go through a process of trial and error as described above. However, just when we think they understand what it is we want, they often seem to lose it or just not do it as well for a while.

When horses are considered as playful creatures that learn through play, it is easy to accept that they will need some time to play with the new exercises we teach them. In other words, their learning curve extends beyond understanding the basic premise to include exploring the limits of the premise. If we don't accept this aspect of their nature then we have no explanation for a horse not repeating an exercise performed and rewarded once, except that he is being willfully resistant. Assuming he is well rested and happy in his work this simply makes no sense. Why would he resist an exercise he finds pleasant and rewarding without reason? More to the point, why would we, without reason, assume he is resisting?

Whether you view the horse as resistant or playful, his manner of learning will remain essentially the same. The difference is in your attitude. If you think your horse is resistant, then you work against him. If you see your horse exploring the rules and limits of the new movement or idea, you explore them with him.

Denying the horse's playful nature and intelligence creates an adversary—a mindless beast that needs to be shown who's boss and forced into submis-

Figure 1 **Horses, like people, have a playful nature and use play to learn.**

sion. All the teachings of the most skillful riders—from Xenophon to the present—are lost to us as the question of the horse being resentful and dull becomes irrelevant, because we become resentful and dull riders. Reject reason and the rules do not work. Training becomes a chaotic hit-or-miss affair. On the other hand, if we can accept the horse's nature and play with him, we make a partner. The rules and reasoning not only work, but work so well, that training takes on a simplicity and symmetry that approaches elegance.

4 Five Rules

Riding and training are more akin to cooking than chemistry, more art than science. Rather than doing an exercise a precise number of times, or using an exact pressure to obtain a result, you have to try a little more or less of this or that, perhaps even invent an approach to a problem that's just a little different. This is the only way to find out what's best for you and your horse because the relationship of horse and rider is as personal and individual as each of its participants. This is the great attraction of riding and, at the same time, its great challenge.

No two people can ever ride exactly the same way any more than they can be exactly the same. A technique that works well for me, a 6'1" man, may not be the best approach for you. Because of this, there is probably no single person that will have all the answers for you. This is not a bad thing because it allows each of us the joy of discovery. We all have the same opportunity to explore the unknown.

Riding and training are more akin to cooking than chemistry, more art than science.

However, there are challenges that individual discovery presents. One is in interpretation. For example, use of a particular phrase that I believe clearly explains my intention is no guarantee my intention will be interpreted correctly by the reader. My use of a phrase that made a difficult concept clear as a bell to me, may add confusion to another. Yet the same concept described in a slightly different manner clears the matter up again.

A second dilemma a rider faces is in separating bad techniques and theories from valid ones. There are many inconsistencies in the riding culture. Some false philosophies and incorrect techniques appear to work at first, but as time passes, a rider discovers they cause more problems than they solve.

There are a lot of bad techniques being thrown around as gospel, but they are not gospel. They are bad techniques.

The good news is there are five simple rules, which either provide a context for the correct interpretation of a valid technique, or allow the rider to determine if a method is not useful. Rather than discussing specific techniques and methods, they provide a framework for interpretation. The five rules provide a basis for the relationship of horse and rider.

Everything written by me can and should be interpreted so that it does not conflict with any of the five rules. If you think a suggested technique or method does conflict with them, I may have said it poorly, or you may have read it incorrectly. However, it is being misunderstood. Every technique I suggest in this book fits within these five rules.

In addition, the rules can and should be used universally. All training techniques and methods from any source, not just me, should fit within them. If a technique cannot be interpreted to fit within the confines of these rules, it's a bad technique. There are a lot of bad techniques being thrown around as gospel, but they are not gospel. They are bad techniques. I certainly do not claim to have managed to fit all training methods between the covers of this book. I do claim, however, that all *valid* training techniques fit within the confines of these five rules.

None of the rules has a higher priority than another. They are all paramount. Nothing else is as important as they are. None of the rules says a particular goal must be achieved on a particular day. However, following the rules does lead to achieving goals that are otherwise elusive. In many cases these five rules will conflict with others that are in common use. In such a situation, ignore the *other* rules.

Rule 1—No One Gets Hurt

"No one gets hurt," because there is no need for anyone to be hurt—ever. Hurt is pain and pain results in the instinctive behavior we are trying to avoid. However, we can use the horse's manner of play to get past aggression and appeal to his intellect.

Horses at play are always kicking, striking, and lashing out with their teeth at one another, yet they almost never make contact. Even when they do, there is a very low percentage of injury, and I have never seen a barefoot horse inflict a serious wound on another (although just because I have not seen it, does not mean it does not happen).

What they do tend to do is shadow box. Actually, it can be fun to watch. They do not follow through with their kicks, strikes, and lashes, they simply demonstrate to one another their respective abilities. By going through the charade of showing the other that, "I could have kicked you here," or, "I really had you nailed that time," they determine the one who would be most likely to avoid injury while inflicting it upon the other. They figure out who is the fastest and most agile and, in so doing, who will be calling the shots.

Horses either have an instinct or have learned to avoid actual combat. Presumably, this is because they are likely to seriously harm each other in a real battle. Since a thirteen-hand pony is capable of doing serious injury to a seventeen-hand horse, all the pony has to do is show the horse he could have kicked him here or there, and that threat is enough in and of itself to win the day. I think of this as the equine equivalent of M.A.D.[1]

If you outmaneuver your horse by moving your hand faster than he can move his body, his natural assumption will be that you are not only quicker than he is, but as strong as he is too.

We can use the horse's characteristic manner of play to get past aggressive behavior. If a horse is trying to kick, bite, or strike out, just remember that he is intimidated by agility and quick, short motions. If you outmaneuver him by moving your hand faster than he can move his body, his natural assumption will be that you are not only quicker than he is, but as strong as

---

1 *"Mutually Assured Destruction" (M.A.D.) was the military policy of the Super Powers during the latter half of the twentieth century. Since each power had enough nuclear warheads to assure the destruction of its opponent, neither side was willing to engage in out-and-out war. All things considered, it was a rather surprisingly good show of horse sense for world leaders.*

he is too. So, if you move as fast as he does, he will begin to slow down and approach in a docile manner. This is really wonderful because a person does not have any chance of overpowering a horse. It is because horses are intimidated by speed alone that a 100-pound woman can intimidate a 1200-hundred pound horse. You don't need to inflict pain to slow him down, just imply it by reacting quickly to aggressive action—simply show your horse that he can be touched, before he can touch.

I do not need to punch a horse in the nose (which is good news since I would probably break my hand!). I can give a quick little tweak and have the same result. In fact, as my goal is to make a play partner out of this creature, I want to be very careful not to cause him pain regardless of how aggressive he is at the outset. I need to show him that I'm not going to hurt him, while at the same time letting him think that I could have. I need to play with him.

My horse will think about me and that is what I want—for him to be thinking and using intellect, instead of instinct.

If I have an aggressive horse, I prefer to have him on the longe line; however, a round pen or square paddock will do as well. Now all I have to do is stay out of his range and lightly touch him with the end of a longe whip to demonstrate that my range extends to him. Very shortly the horse decides to give up the fight and take to flight. If he is on the longe, in a pen or paddock, he has a problem. He isn't going anywhere.

Next, I wait for him to realize that. When he does, he will stop running, turn, and look at me. He will think about me and that is what I want—for him to be thinking and using intellect instead of instinct. Although I'm not yet physically safe, I can begin to show him that he is safe with me, that nothing bad is ever going to happen to him while I'm around. Once he starts to understand that, I begin to become safe with him around me. I can then teach him how to play with me. In time, I'll be able to rely on him for my safety, and he on me for his.

It is important to note that "hurting" is not the same as "making uncomfortable." "Hurt" implies injury and pain—stepping on glass with bare feet for example. Discomfort is not painful, but it's not pleasant either, sort of like sitting in a lumpy chair. Rather than sitting there and being uncomfortable, it's natural to try and find another chair. Another way of comparing the two is to remember that *pain* remains, while *discomfort* disappears when its source is removed.

The distinction between "hurt" and "discomfort" is important because there are occasions when we need make a horse a little uncomfortable in order to prevent him from hurting himself. For instance, the horse is always better off when the rider quietly, but firmly, insists that he go correctly even if it means a little discomfort at the outset, because failing to develop the horse's muscles properly leads to a bad back and arthritic hocks.

There are times when we need to encourage our horses to do the right thing, or make it uncomfortable for them to do the wrong thing. But it's important to remember we never fix anything with pain. When we use speed instead of strength and some occasional discomfort if required, we appeal to the horse's intellect rather than his instinct. Using his capacity to learn, we play with him on terms he understands. In time, the horse realizes that he is safe with us and begins to look to us for security and guidance. This cornerstone of the relationship should never be disregarded.

There are times when we need to encourage our horses to do the right thing, or make it uncomfortable for them to do the wrong thing. But it's important to remember we never fix anything with pain.

Rule 2—Reward In Proportion

Reward is the only way we can appeal to the horse's intellect and the only positive way the horse has to figure out what we are asking of him. When reward is used correctly, the horse accepts the rider as leader and learns to rely on him for guidance. But in order to use reward at all the horse must first be taught about it, as reward is not as simple as it seems.

When a horse performs well and the rider gives him a rest, and perhaps some praise, that is a *reward*. If a rider is considerate of his partner and consistent in his reward, then in time, the horse discovers that performing the exercise correctly is a pleasant experience for him as well. That is the *reward of the exercise*. However, if the horse is overworked and left unrewarded, he learns to seek relief in his own way.

The rule this chapter is named for, *Reward in Proportion,* is the positive form of the old saying, "Don't snatch a defeat from the jaws of victory." Simply put it means the more difficult the exercise is for the horse, the more frequently he should be rewarded or else you are going to confuse the horse instead of train him. This is true whether the difficulty is in the physical demands of a movement or exercise he's familiar with, or if the horse is trying to figure out something new you are asking for.

In the situation of teaching the horse something new, as soon as he offers some indication he's beginning to understand, reward him even if he does not offer all that you want. Let's take my earlier example of teaching a horse to move from the whip (p. 13). If at first the horse kicks out but then just lifts his leg without either kicking or moving it away, I reward him at that moment. Then I take a few minutes to repeat the exercise, until he accepts the idea that he should quietly lift his leg when I touch him with the whip. At this point it is easy enough to get him to lift his leg and move it away (my original goal) by just giving him a gentle nudge on his flank.

...as soon as the horse offers some indication he's beginning to understand, reward him even if he does not offer all that you want.

By keeping the reward proportionate to the horse's understanding, I am able to achieve my goal in just a few minutes. In fact, almost anyone can teach almost any horse just about anything this basic in just as little time—as long as he or she rewards proportionately. Conversely, by failing to reward little improvements, even training simple tasks can be difficult.

To see how such an easy training task can become difficult, let's go back to the example I mentioned above and look at it a different way. The trainer is attempting to teach a horse to move quietly away from the whip. The horse is still in the trial-and-error stage, trying to figure out what is wanted, so he reacts typically and kicks out, backs up, and tries to walk through the hand. Throughout all of this, the trainer quietly ignores the incorrect responses and continues to ask the horse to keep trying to figure it out. Then, when the horse does just quietly lift his leg, the trainer decides that is not enough and instead of rewarding he continues to tap the horse's leg in hope the horse will give him more and move it over too.

Well, the horse might figure it out and move his leg over, or, he might decide to go through his list of options again with more force. So, this time he kicks out harder, tries to pull through the reins with more determination, or backs away from the trainer much faster than he did before. He may even decide that he is going to plant all four feet on the ground and not move them no matter what the trainer does. The one thing he almost certainly won't do again is just quietly lift his foot. He won't try that again right now because he just did it and the trainer, by his action of continuing to ask for more, told him that is not what was wanted.

So, although the horse offers the trainer an opportunity to reward a small improvement, the trainer misses his chance and now he is worse off than before he started—now his horse is less inclined to do what is wanted. And that is what I mean when I say "reward in proportion" or risk "snatching a defeat from the jaws of victory."

In addition to how often the reward is given, the reward must be long enough to fully rest the horse. Young, green, or incorrectly ridden horses all lack the muscle to find any exercise very easy. By the same token, a well-muscled horse learning advanced work is doing more difficult and strenuous tasks. In every situation, the reward must be in proportion to the exercise: the more difficult the horse finds the exercise to perform, the less of the exercise should be requested before reward is offered, and, the reward must be a true rest period so the horse is not asked to perform in a sore and tired state. The horse is the best judge of how much rest is required. If he is having a good time and enjoying his work, he actually begins again on his own. No, he will not run through an entire dressage test again, but if he has been working and then allowed a rest, he will perk up and signal when he is ready to restart.

Young, green, or incorrectly ridden horses all lack the muscles to find any exercise very easy.

Reward in proportion helps determine how often to reward and for how long; however, the immediacy of reward must be considered as well. For the horse to associate the reward with doing an exercise correctly, there cannot be any other requests made before the reward is offered. Going back to my early example of teaching a dog to sit, imagine how much more complicated this endeavor would be if, after the dog sat, he was made to come to the trainer before being rewarded. The poor dog wouldn't know whether the reward was being offered for having sat or for having approached the trainer. It's just as confusing when the horse has figured out an exercise and performed it, and then the rider demands a halt, or worse yet, hauls on his mouth to stop him before rewarding. The horse doesn't know what the rider wants.

Rewarding a puppy correctly for sitting on command is a simple matter. Walk up to him and praise him. It is also fairly simple to reward a horse that is standing quietly. However, rewarding a horse *in motion* is more complex since you are still telling him how fast and where to go. In order to have the horse understand that he can stop, rest, and accept reward immediately, he has to be taught when it is appropriate. That is why the *Allowed Stop* is incorporated into the first lesson as well as all others throughout the career of the horse.

The *Allowed Stop* is simply what its name implies: the horse is allowed to stop the exercise and rest. So, when I wish to reward my horse, I drop the reins on his neck, pat him, and say, "Good boy. Whoa." Since the horse has had this series of actions and words impressed upon him since his first lessons with me, he knows that he is being rewarded and can relax and enjoy his accomplishment for a few moments or minutes. It is more than reward—it is instantaneous reward. But the Allowed Stop must be taught. Although many horse and rider combinations seem to work it out over time, the time spent training until they do is not of much value.

With the acceptance of reward, the horse has elected his rider as boss.

With the acceptance of reward, the horse has elected his rider as boss. The horse will learn that reward comes from figuring out what it is we want. An interesting symmetry of nature is that as the horse relies more on us for reward, rest, and guidance, we in turn can rely more and more on the horse. The horse becomes reliable. The more the horse trusts that no harm will come to him while we are around and that our demands will not exceed his limits, the more trustworthy he becomes. This circular relationship evolves only when we rely on the horse for guidance to his limits. We need to trust him when he says he has forgotten, had enough, or does not understand.

The more the horse trusts that no harm will come to him while we are around, and that our demands will not exceed his limits, the more trustworthy he becomes.

In addition to the reward that *we* give, the horse discovers the reward of the exercise. Horses enjoy the feeling of a good workout, just as we find that doing any athletic activity well feels good to us. Playing tennis, running a race, skiing, or working out in a gym are all good examples. After any athletic activity, your muscles should feel used, but not abused. You might be tired perhaps but relaxed—not defeated. You should have a pleasant memory of having done something better than before and be looking forward to doing it again. It's this feeling of being on top of your game that is the reward of the exercise. This is how a horse should feel when brought back to his stall. Not sometimes—every time!

To attain this rewarding feeling, a good coach is required, one that instills a love of the game first and lets winning the game take care of itself. A good coach will take the time to explain the fundamentals then he'll ask for slow and easy practice until the student develops skill and coordination. If the student gets tired, he'll rest him. If the student becomes frustrated, the coach will reduce the difficulty of the exercise. This coach's student won't have to be pushed or cajoled into performing. He'll become addicted to the rewarding feeling of having performed well and strive to do better just for that feeling alone.

Horses get this love-of-the-game attitude from carrying a rider well. I see it in them all the time. A good example is a horse that has been "falling in" for years. Invariably, when he first discovers how to bend and stay perpendicular to the ground going around corners, he will breathe a sigh of relief and start to play with his legs, enjoying the feeling of moving correctly. This concept is true for any well-ridden figure or movement. When the horse uses his body correctly, carrying us becomes pleasant and rewarding. If riding well feels good to us, carrying a rider well must feel great to the horse!

Of course, when it comes to riding, the rider is equivalent to the coach, and the horse the student. Unfortunately not all riders have the attitude of the coach I described. All too many riders put the game before the love of the game. Rather than observing the horse to see if he's tired, they look at the clock. If the horse complains that an exercise is too difficult, they hit him with a stick, poke him with a spur, or pull on his mouth and, to make matters worse, when he does get it right, they forget to reward. A horse faced with this will hate being ridden, avoid the rider, and learn to be defensive as he tries to protect himself.

Making a horse defensive is really a simple matter; anyone can do it, just work him too hard.

Making a horse defensive is really a simple matter; anyone can do it, just work him too hard. A young horse trying to figure out how to balance himself by taking more weight on the inside hind leg can only do it for so long. Work him past his limit, and he will resort to trial and error to figure out a way to rest that leg. At some point, he will lean on a hand. His burden is reduced: relief, immediate reward. This not only teaches him to lean, but it also teaches him the more damning lesson—he can find his own reward by figuring out how to protect himself. The rider did not reward him when he leaned on the hand—the horse gave it to himself. If the rider corrects with no reward, then another defense is tried. More correction, more defenses... Without a radical change, the horse will develop defenses faster than corrections can be created. When this happens, the rider becomes frustrated, and correction is replaced by punishment. Then the horse is only concerned with protecting himself, the exercise-reward cycle is broken, and it is impossible to teach anything.

Riding masters of the past understood the power of rewarding even the smallest improvement in a horse's effort—perhaps that's why they spoke so often of a horse's generous nature, willingness, and intelligence. They also understood the results of failing to reward. They would say a horse had been "spoiled" or "ruined"—their very choice of words suggesting a person had done it to the horse.. Less knowledgeable riders lay the blame on the horse and call him resistant, evasive, willful, stubborn, stupid or crazy.

When all is said and done, you have no choice in this matter. Fail to keep your horse reliant on you for rest, reward, and guidance and he will become oblivious to your aids, determining for himself how best to deal with the requirements of being ridden. On the other hand, when you reward correctly, your horse will discover that you both have the same goals. He'll decide that being ridden on a daily basis is fun, and working with you is rewarding not only because of the reward you give, but because the game is rewarding in and of itself.

> *Fail to keep your horse reliant on you for rest, reward, and guidance and he will determine for himself how to deal with being ridden.*

Rule 3—Every Step Counts

Make every step the horse takes contribute to his development. Do not allow the horse to go badly. This rule does not require the horse to perform as if he is going down the centerline at the Olympics every moment under saddle. It does require that the horse softens in his jaw, poll and neck to the hand and seat, and softens throughout his body to the seat and leg.

When softness and relaxation are the top priority in training, precision, accuracy, free forward movement, engagement, cadence, and impulsion will develop on their own. Softness is analogous to having relaxed muscles. When a horse is soft, he is physically malleable. By touching here and pressing there he can be shaped.

Softness is not the same as lightness. Two pieces of wood can be touching lightly; however, that does not make the wood soft or the contact between them elastic. Softness manifests itself in a horse that is elastic and supple. (See p. 36 for more discussion on softness).

Asking the horse to stretch or compress his body, bend his joints, and swing his back is asking for elasticity within the horse. Muscles cannot be elastic and in a state of tension at the same time. A horse cannot yield to the hand and pull against it simultaneously, nor can he stiffen against a leg while bending away from it. This internal relaxation—the softening and giving of muscles—takes priority over the movement.

In contrast to a horse being *on the aids* and softening to them, he can be *against the aids* or, as is sometimes said, *running through the aids*. A horse that is running through the rein aid will physically stiffen his muscles and pull against it instead of softening in his jaw and poll. Usually when this happens, the horse's tempo and speed will get faster. A horse that is against the leg will move into it instead of softening and moving away from it. Yet another term to describe a horse against the aids is *behind the aids*. When a horse is behind the leg, instead of increasing his engagement or moving forward, he will "suck back" and decrease his energy output when the rider puts his legs on.

Teaching the horse to soften to the aids is a daily part of riding. Softening exercises should be reviewed at the beginning of every ride, everyday, and whenever the horse requires them during the ride. Everything in riding is based upon the horse softening to the aids. The advanced movements seen in Grand Prix dressage are nothing more than a test of how confirmed the horse's softening response is. For example, if a horse stiffens when asked for a piaffe, the best to be hoped for is that he lift his legs in some sort of rhythm. Without softness a free-swinging piaffe with the back undulating and the presence of cadence is impossible. If the horse does not soften to the aids, whatever you are working on must be abandoned for a few moments while softness and relaxation are reestablished. I often say to my students in these situations, "Stick with your horse, not the exercise."

Everything in riding is based upon the horse softening to the aids.

By keeping softness as the paramount goal, every use of the aids becomes a reminder and request to the horse to stay soft. Softness is the first prerequisite to being, *on the aids*. For a horse to be truly on the aids, he must be developed physically and mentally so he is capable of always being engaged and balanced, with his back up and swinging. Ideally, horses are always on the aids; however, that is the ideal. Here we deal with the reality of training.

There are times in training when it is not possible to have as much energy or freedom as you would like. In many situations—when you introduce a new exercise for example—it may not even be desirable. However, the horse should always work quietly and softly. When training, it does no good to have a horse perform an exercise if he does so with stiffness and tension. While it is possible to have a horse present a movement that appears to be a shoulder-in, without relaxation, the benefit of the exercise is lost.

There is only one circumstance where riding in stiffness may be valid—when the rider is attempting to ride through the stiffness. In this case, the horse may be asked to continue the exercise for a brief period. The moment the horse softens, or even begins to soften, the exercise is ended and reward offered. In other words, the priority has shifted from performing a shoulder-in, to softening to the aids for shoulder-in. In this way the horse will learn to soften in response to the aids for the exercise. It is only when the horse has learned to soften to the aids as he begins the exercise that a second or third step done in softness may be requested.

When this concept is applied to all exercises, they will be done with lightness and balance. Energy and freedom will follow of their own accord. Just remember, one good step is better than ten thousand bad ones.

Rule 4—Correction, Not Punishment

Just remember, one good step is better than ten thousand bad ones.

Correction says, "Do this," and ends in a reward. Punishment says, "Don't do that!" and just ends. Correction comes from knowledge, is rational, and deals with problems rather than symptoms. Punishment comes from frustration, is emotional, and almost always deals with the symptoms rather than the core problems.

A good correction is *clear, effective,* and *over with.* To be clear, it must be distinct, unambiguous, and easily understood. To be effective, it must be sufficiently compelling that its purpose is accomplished within a reasonable time, so that it can be *over with*—you stop using it and reward.

A good correction is clear, effective, *and* over with.

To be clear and effective, you must be able look past the symptom and find the problem. Figuring out the difference between symptoms and problems isn't that difficult when you simplify instead of qualify.

For example, when someone says, "My horse spooks in the corner," don't qualify "spooking" with the phrase, "in the corner." Simplify it! Say, "My horse spooks." As you will soon see, dealing with a horse that spooks is straightforward. Trying to sort out why a particular horse spooks in one corner but not others, and why other horses spook in different corners but not this one will make you crazy! By the time you're done analyzing corners, you're so far removed from the problem you'll never figure it out.

So don't qualify problems with statements like, "My horse falls out at the gate," or, "My horse bucks when the wind blows." Simplify these complaints to, "My horse falls out," or "My horse bucks." You need to simplify because qualified complaints are infinite. There's at least one for every real or imagined distraction on the planet!

By simplifying instead of qualifying, you go from an infinite number of complaints to a grand total of seven: a horse can misbehave under saddle by rearing, bucking, spooking, bolting, stopping, falling in or out. All these problems always trace back to the horse not being soft, and a lack of softness is just the horse saying he does not understand his basics well enough. To fix this, review the basics—from the ground up if necessary. As much of the rest of this book describes how to teach your horse good basics, you'll be well equipped to deal with any difficulties you encounter.

When you can see past the symptoms to the problems you are faced with and have the tools to deal with them, you'll find that no matter how bad things used to seem, your corrections are now made with a generous and helpful attitude. You'll never feel a need to punish, get angry, or inflict pain. When your corrections are intended to help your horse stay soft, relaxed, and in balance, they build the relationship. Punishment destroys it.

Rule 5—Take Your Time

In essence, this rule really just says to take the time to follow all the other rules. How much time? Well, it could be moments or it could be months, but that isn't important. It's important that the rules are followed, not how long the process takes. It is not necessary to fix everything today; in fact, it's not necessary to fix anything today.

Many repetitions followed by positive reinforcement are required for true learning.

A strongly ingrained notion of the equestrian culture is that corrections must be made immediately. The theory is that unless the horse is promptly punished for aberrant behavior, he will learn that he can "get away with it" and forever be spoiled as a mount. Nonsense! Horses do not learn after only one or two repetitions of any behavior. Many repetitions followed by positive reinforcement are required for true learning—whether it's good or bad. Otherwise, Grand Prix horses would be made in a week.

Yes, of course it's "best" to always correct a problem as it occurs and end on a good note; however, there will be times when the solution eludes us and the ride just has to end. There's no rush. Training problems are like dinner dishes left in the sink; they're still there in the morning. Keep that in mind and take a night to ponder a new approach or two. The problem may prove much less severe tomorrow.

Problems really come in only two varieties, technical and behavioral. A technical problem consists of difficulty teaching something new. Although riders sometimes become frustrated because a horse doesn't understand a particular training method, I think these problems are actually fun. They are opportunities to figure out new, and often better, methods. Many of the training techniques I describe later in this book are simply the result of my having had to figure out a different approach to get a horse to understand a new concept.

To fix behavioral problems, just remind your horse that he is supposed to soften to the hand and leg, then you can help him find his balance again and you'll be amazed at how quickly these problems disappear.

Regardless of the nature of the specific problem, the procedure to fix it remains the same. First, figure out which basic you think is going wrong and then pick an exercise with a reasonable chance to fix it. For example, if a horse continually ends up by the in-gate when he's supposed to be doing school figures, he's not running for the gate (although it may seem that way), he's falling out. Take a few minutes to fix the falling out and then go back to riding the figures. A horse that is anticipating or getting worried about flying changes may be picking up speed and trying to rush through the change. He is rushing through the aids. Forget about the changes for a while, follow Rule Number 3 and make the horse soft again. Perhaps work on half-halts, counter bend in the canter, maybe even some canter-walk transitions followed by some simple changes. When the horse will canter across the diagonal and half-halt in response to just a touch of your seat, he is ready to try a flying change again.

Rather than worrying about accomplishing things today, look at the big picture.

Rather than worry about accomplishing things today, look at the big picture. A well-trained horse should be useful until well into his twenties. Whether he is a youngster or a teenager, spending a few minutes, days, or weeks to find and correct the root of a problem should return years of use and enjoyment. I don't know of a better investment of time and effort. It's like putting a hundred dollars into a bank account once and then being able to withdraw a hundred dollars from it whenever you want and as often as you want for the next ten or twelve years. There is another benefit too. It is quite impossible to solve a behavioral or technical problem without learning something new or arriving at a deeper understanding of the basics. So by taking enough time to figure things out and fix them correctly, you not only make your horse a better horse for the rest of his life but you make yourself a better rider for the rest of yours.

Taking the time to fix things correctly is not the same as being patient. I'm not patient—Hell, I'm the most impatient person I know. Surprisingly I'm always accused of being patient with horses but I'm not. Really! I'm not. If a horse I'm working with needs correction, I'll try an exercise and give it less than 30 seconds to begin to work. I decide if the exercise is working by observing the horse's reaction. If I see him learning in a methodical manner and trying to figure out my request through trial and error, I continue. If he's not, I change my approach. That's not patience!

Patience was personified for me by a middle-aged woman trotting endlessly around a 20-meter circle hoping for the day when her horse would magically decide to perform as she dreamed. It never occurred to her that she was completely ineffective and needed to change her technique and approach. Now that's patience. That got her nowhere. She was not reacting to her horse and her horse was not reacting to her. It reminded me of Struther Martin's famous line from the movie *Cool Hand Luke,* "What we got heeere...is failure...to communicate."

Patience implies you have to be patient with the horse, as though there is something wrong or missing with him. That's not needed. Horses go well when they are well ridden. If riders need patience, they need it with themselves. It takes time to learn proper training techniques and develop good riding skills. Once they are there, the horse responds accordingly.

So, if you find yourself stuck at some problem or point of training, just take the time to evaluate the situation using these five rules, and then by using these rules again figure out a solution. Borrow a bit of horse sense from your partner and apply some trial and error to your methods until you find out how to get back on track. As long as you stay within the limits of these rules, you'll be fine.

PART TWO

On Horseback in a Physical World

5 Terms

The way we talk about riding shapes the way we think about riding and ultimately the way we ride. If the words used don't mean what they say or are used incorrectly, they just confuse, confound, and frustrate. Then, we end up saying it wrong, thinking it wrong, and doing it wrong. Frequent comments about our failure to communicate with each other are, "Well, you have to feel it to understand it," or, "It's like trying to describe the color blue to a blind man."

Of course there will never be a substitute for experience, but we owe it to our horses (and to ourselves) to try to be precise in our language and thinking. Learning to ride is difficult enough without the use of terms that are awkward, obtuse, and contrary. The various terms and phrases used in riding are interrelated and understanding them is a necessary element for success.

Because these terms are interrelated, it is difficult to discuss them individually, so I've put them into groups. Of course, these are not all the words that are necessary to discuss the

The way we talk about riding shapes the way we think about riding and ultimately the way we ride.

training of horses, just the ones that we need to begin with or that I can describe in a few sentences. This chapter also deals with some inconsistent terms and some terms with inconsistent meaning that are in common usage. Some words and phrases, *contact* and *direction, angle, and bend* for example, need entire chapters to be discussed which I do later on.

Softness, Lightness, Stretch, and Elasticity

Softness is the ability to absorb energy without returning it. A quality of softness in this context is malleability. A soft horse can be formed, put in a shape, and left there for a few moments. When a horse is soft, the inside rein can be dropped for a few strides without loss of frame or bend. By starting with softness, the qualities of lightness, stretch, and elasticity can be attained.

> *A soft horse can be formed, put in a shape, and left there for a few moments.*

Lightness can be defined as responsiveness. When a horse understands the rider's aids and responds to them quickly and easily, he is light. However, responsiveness by itself is not sufficient for correct riding. A horse can be responsive and light but stiff as a rail.

The word "*stretch,*" as used in riding, can be defined as the horse's desire to be in a comfortable frame. A horse that knows how to accept the bit will always stretch into the hand instead of remaining over-flexed, cramped, or hollow. Getting a horse to stretch is not a question of how to make him do so, but a matter of showing him that he is allowed to. If a horse does not stretch once he understands he is allowed to, it is because the rider is holding on too tightly.

Stretching and *pulling* are often confused. When a horse is stretching to the bit, he will still respond to the rider's hands, soften, and bend. A horse that is pulling will not. He will tend to stiffen in response to an action of the rider's hand. A stretching horse bends, a pulling horse cannot.

Elasticity is a combination of softness, lightness, and stretch. The word elasticity has a degree of tension implicit in it. Correctly interpreted, the tension required for elasticity is positive.

Think of a rubber band lying on a table. It obviously has the ability to absorb and return energy. Stretching it, puts energy in, and releasing it, returns the energy. Just lying there on the table, completely limp, it has potential to accept energy, but no energy to return. Conversely, pulled to its maximum limit, when it is under complete tension, it can release energy but cannot accept anymore. As it approaches its breaking point, rather then feeling elastic, it feels like string or rope. It vibrates when tweaked. Only when the rubber band is stretched to a place comfortably within its limits does it remain elastic. A point where it still has the ability to absorb energy without reaching its maximum limit and release energy without becoming limp, defines elastic in the sense we use the word.

It is a balance of softness and tension that creates the elasticity we seek. When these qualities are in balance, the horse stretches into the hand, but does not pull on it. The relative amount of softness versus tension in the horse is the difference between a dull, tense, or brilliant performance. The difference in softness and tension in various parts of the horse creates the balance we are looking for.

This balance is definable. There should be virtually no tension in the jaw and very little in the poll. The jaw and poll should be soft, accepting energy but not returning it. There should be just enough tension so that the horse keeps his mouth easily closed and holds his head in a comfortable position. How much tension in your jaw and neck do you have sitting and reading this book? That is equivalent to the amount of tension there should be in the horse's jaw and poll. (A rider relying upon a tight noseband to keep his horse's mouth closed is doing something very drastically wrong.)

The horse's back should be in a mid-range of elasticity, not so loose that it lies on the table like a rubber band and not so tight that is pulled to the maximum. It should accept and return energy easily.

Energy comes from the horse, but relaxation is taught and then allowed by the rider. A horse has to learn to soften to the hand by yielding in the jaw, poll, and neck, and to soften to the leg by bending and stepping away from it. Once the horse understands that, the various degrees of elasticity required throughout the rest of the body is his responsibility. The horse will figure it out, because doing so is the easiest and most enjoyable way to carry a rider.

Energy comes from the horse, but relaxation is taught and then allowed by the rider.

Direction

Your *direction* is defined by the line that you're moving on. It's your line of travel. If you're going on a circle, or curve—your line of travel is the circumference of the circle, or curve. Direction can be used to influence angle and bend.

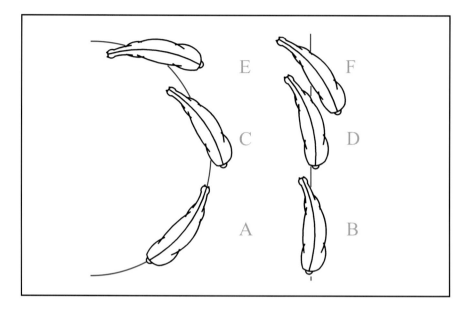

Figure 2 On a circle and a straight line, this drawing illustrates horses on their lines of travel (A and B); at a little angle to their lines (C and D); and with more angle to their lines (E and F).

Angle

If your horse's front and rear feet are equal distance to his line of travel, he is on his line of travel, or *on his line* (fig. 2, A and B). This is true whether on a straight line such as a long side or diagonal, or on a curve such as a circle or corner. When a horse is moving laterally, he has an *angle to his line* He can have a little angle (fig. 2, C and D), or he can have more angle (fig. 2, E and F).

Bend

Bend refers to the lateral bend of the horse as can be viewed from above (fig. 3). Ideally, a horse will have a single, continuous, even bend from his poll to his dock. I say a horse with no bend, *has no bend.* I don't use the word *straight* to describe this because the dressage world already uses the word *straight* to describe a horse with an *even bend.* A horse is over bent if he has more bend in his neck and at the withers, than in his body. When on a horse that's over bent it feels as if his withers are in front of your hip instead of right in front of your belly button as it feels on a horse with an even bend (fig. 4).

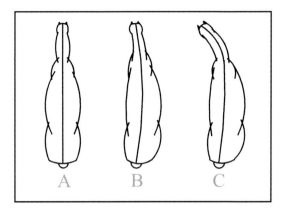

Figure 3 The lateral bend of a horse (seen from above): a horse with no bend (A); even bend from poll to dock (B); and over bent with too much bend in his neck (C).

Figure 4 A horse with an even bend on a straight line: Boogie is evenly bent from poll to dock, and on his line of travel.

Collection, Engagement, and Elevation

The essence of *collection* is that the horse is moving in a manner that allows change most freely. For example, a horse performing collected canter can on any given stride be asked for an extension, halt, flying change, or pirouette.

In order to be able move this way he has to be engaged. *Engagement* occurs when the horse's hind legs move so the hocks travel from point of buttocks forward and bend equally in the stifle, hock, and ankle. This allows more weight to be taken on the hind legs, which the horse counter-balances by raising his head and neck. The shift of weight to the rear legs and the subsequent higher head position allows the forelegs to take higher, rounded, more lofty steps. When the horse has raised his head and neck position and is taking rounded steps with his forelegs, he is said to be *elevated*.

Often people confuse the *function* of collection—with the *frame* seen in collection. The *frame* is the silhouette of the horse as seen from the side. When this confusion occurs, the rider attempts to elevate the forehand with the reins and actually prevents the horse from bringing his legs underneath and engaging.

Avoiding the pitfall of trying to pull the horse's head up with the reins requires a small act of faith. The rider has to believe that the horse is capable of adjusting his own frame in order to keep his own balance. When the rider insists the horse remains soft, while at the same time allowing the horse to select his own frame, the horse develops a *topline*—the muscles along the top of the horse's spine develop and become more rounded. As the topline develops the horse becomes more engaged and then offers true elevation on his own (fig. 5).

Gait, Rhythm, Tempo, and Speed

Horses have three basic *gaits*, walk, trot, and canter. The *rhythm* is determined by the number of footfalls per stride in each of the gaits. This means the words gait and rhythm are nearly the same: the walk has a rhythm of four beats per stride because each of the horse's feet hit the ground consecutively. The rhythm of the trot is two beats per stride since the feet hit the ground in diagonal pairs, and the rhythm of the canter has three beats.

The *tempo* is the number of beats per minute. Tempo and length of stride determine speed. For example, a horse can travel at the speed of ten miles per hour by taking short strides quickly (fast tempo) or by taking longer strides more slowly (moderate tempo).

Figure 5 This horse is in collection. His right hind leg demonstrates engagement—
equal bend of the three joints, with the leg moving from the point of the horse's
buttocks forward. The height of his poll shows his elevation. He is taking more
weight on his hind legs, thus freeing up his forehand. Note this horse's stride
remains free-swinging and rhythmical.

Inside and Outside

Since we are going to be dealing with bending horses to the right or left for
the remainder of the book, this seems an appropriate place to clarify a little
terminology about the inside and outside of the horse. The *inside* of the horse
is the side to which he is bent. If the horse is bent to his left, his left side is

called his inside, the left rein is the inside rein, the rider's left leg is the rider's inside leg, and the horse's left legs are his inside hind and forelegs. Following the same logic, the *outside* is the side the horse is bent away from. If the horse is bent to the left, the horse's right side is the outside of the horse, the right rein is the outside rein, the rider's right leg is the riders outside leg, and the horse's right legs are his outside hind and forelegs.

Still, Stiff, and Soft Hands

...hands cannot be "kept" still—they have to be "allowed" to be still.

What we think of as still or quiet hands are actually "apparently" still. That is, the hands are *still* relative to the horse's movement but are moving a substantial amount relative to the rider's seat and back, which take up the motion of the horse. For this reason, hands cannot be "kept" still—they have to be "allowed" to be still.

For hands to be soft and appear still, the rider's shoulders and elbows have to be disconnected from the seat (except for brief moments when the hands are used in conjunction with a braced back). This is accomplished by allowing the shoulders to relax completely so that the upper arm simply hangs, then the elbow is bent enough to keep a straight line from bit to elbow.

A rider who allows his arms to fall into this comfortable position will have hands that will feel soft and relaxed to the horse. If the horse has been trained enough to keep his balance, and use the reins only for guides, the picture will be of a quiet horse and a rider with still hands.

However, if a horse is pulling or leaning on the hands, and the rider attempts to force his hands to remain in the same position, the hands are stiff. The more the hands stiffen against the horse, the more the horse pulls, and the cycle continues until there is nothing left but a strength contest. When the rider attempts to force quiet hands, a tension is put into the elbows, which transfers to the shoulders, and then goes into the back and begins to lock up the seat. All this tension creates a stiff rider and a stiff horse.

So, if the horse begins to pull the hands from their natural position, the rider can brace his back for a stride or two in order to restore correct contact. However, if the horse isn't sufficiently trained to yield and engage within a stride or two, then any attempt to prevent the hands from moving results in a tug of war. Instead, the exercise must be abandoned while the rider does what is necessary to make the horse soft again. If this includes moving hands, that's fine. Then, when the horse is soft again, return to the exercise with still, soft hands.

6

The Aids of Reason

Aids request, encourage, and allow. They differ from corrections that are clear, effective, and over with; and from rewards which are immediate and proportional. In terms of the exercise-reward cycle, aids are used to ask correctly, corrections are used to make correct, and rewards are used to reward.

Aids change as the horse's training progresses because implicit in the word training is the word *changing*. We expect the horse to change as a result of training, so as he does, the way we ride him and use our aids has to change. Ideally, when riding a fully trained horse, it seems as though we don't use any aids at all, that we merely sit there and think about what we want. To get to that ideal, we have to ride green horses with more deliberate aids for a while. The aids a very green horse needs, will of necessity be different from the ideal of sitting quietly on the fully trained horse.

When riding a green horse on the aids, we guide his gait, direction, angle, frame, bend, tempo, length of stride, and energy. That's a lot! Too much to deal with in any one

...implicit in the word training is the word changing.

moment. In fact, it's too much to deal with each item individually. However, you'll see in Part Three, *That Delicate Balance,* because of the way they are related to each other, we can adjust one or two in a stride and then others in the next—very much the way a juggler keeps several objects in the air with only two hands.

Juggling depends on tempo and rhythm. A juggler only has so much time to catch an object and toss it up again before the next one falls. The same is true for "juggling" the horse's gait, direction, angle, frame, bend, tempo, length of stride, and energy. When riding on the aids, you have to make one adjustment and then go on to the next before something else falls apart. As a practical matter in riding, this means an aid has to be applied and released within the time of a single stride, so to use hands, seat and legs as aids, you must use them in the tempo and rhythm of the horse.

Force of the Aids

The tempo and rhythm of the aids largely determine the scope and force of the aids. When using aids in the horse's tempo, there just isn't enough time to apply big or strong, powerful aids. For demonstration, clap your hands lightly in the tempo of a horse trotting. Notice that you only move your hands an inch or two on each beat. Now, try to maintain the same tempo while moving your hands much farther apart. It can't be done. Next, see if you can keep the trot tempo while clapping loudly, forcefully. Again, the tempo is lost.

This little demonstration shows how slight an aid must be—a mere bump of the calf, a touch of the spur. Riding on the aids requires such a light touch! Grab the rein too strongly, and you've lost the rhythm—you're riding the next stride already. When everything is going very well, the aids are like fingers drumming on the table: one two three, one two three, one two three...

Request, Encourage, and Allow

Because we only have a moment to fix one thing before we're off to adjust the next, the aids have to be requests that encourage and allow. There simply isn't enough time for the aids to be so strong that they're physically compelling. In fact, there really isn't enough time for the aids to be commands. Rather, the aids are conversational—like a good salesman who leads a customer down his path by asking all the right questions and then agreeing with everything the customer says.

However, even the best salesman needs a customer who understands the questions. So, you have to teach your horse what it is you are asking of him. If you want your legs to mean "please go," you have to teach your horse that when you touch him with your legs, you are asking him to go.

No Mechanical Effects

We have to teach horses what the aids mean because the hand, seat, and leg have, in and of themselves, no meaning, and virtually no mechanical effect upon the horse. If they did we would not have to train horses, only riders.

Many examples of hand, seat, and leg having the opposite effect than intended prove this point. When jumping a "rusher," the hands have no stopping effect at all. Indeed, the more you pull on the reins, the more likely the horse is to increase speed as he approaches the fence. They actually teach racehorses to pull on the hands and go as fast as they can, and a jockey's legs are never in contact with the horse's sides. A trained horse may move away from the leg, but an improperly schooled or green horse is as likely to move into it. Finally, the only natural instinct a horse has to weight on its back is to buck it off.

Thinking of aids as more than requests but as physical forces that actually push our horses forward, sideways, or up to the bit and into the hand is just plain wrong. They do not. A horse will move forward in response to legs because he has learned to associate the rider's legs as a request to go forward. If he does go, it is because he likes to go and wants to please. Ride a horse with the attitude that you make him go with strong legs, or control him with your hands, and he will eventually stop going altogether. At best, he will become shut off and frustrated. "Pushing" a horse that has been "shut off" from the aids with strong legs is futile. Better to get off, stand behind him, and push on his backside, because the more leg used, the more rigid he will become.

The hand, seat, and leg have, in and of themselves, no meaning, and virtually no mechanical effect upon the horse. If they did we would not have to train horses, only riders.

Meaning and Silence

For our horses to understand the aids, the aids have to be consistent throughout training. They must mean the same thing in the walk, trot, and canter—

whether riding figures such as a circle, serpentine and lines, a course of fences, or performing dressage movements like the shoulder-in, half-pass, and pirouette. This isn't as complicated as it seems. It boils down to soften, bend, and move into the hand. That is all the aids ever actually say. When viewed in this context, the various figures and movements are merely demonstrations of how well the horse understands this basic idea.

...soften, bend, and move into the hand. That is all the aids ever actually say.

Since the aids are requests, they should be clear and isolated. There have to be moments of silence when we are not using any aids at all. Just as I need punctuation to separate the thoughts on this page so you can understand what I'm writing, a horse needs moments of silence to separate one aid from the next. Without moments of silence the aids become an indecipherable din of background noise that he doesn't pay any attention to.

We have to use aids that encourage and allow as well as make requests that are clear and consistent. Basically, using aids that encourage and allow is a question of using aids that make sense. Obviously, the aids should not prevent the horse from performing what we are asking him to do. For example, if we want him to stretch into the hand we cannot hold the reins so tightly they prevent him from stretching.

If we want the horse to carry us lightly forward in a flowing and graceful manner, we cannot use aids that make him nervous and tense. To create elegant movement, a light touch of the leg is appropriate. If we grab the horse with our legs or poke him in the ribs with spurs then he will tighten the muscles in his ribcage, which discourages him from moving freely.

Aids that allow are released at least once per stride. An aid held for longer than that becomes a hindrance. A rein aid that remains on for more than a stride or two becomes a "head rest." Rather than softening to it, the horse will lean on or brace against it.

For an aid to be genuinely encouraging, it has to be applied at just the right moment of each stride. There are several good examples of this. The most common would be when asking for lateral movement. Here, it makes the most sense and is the most encouraging to the horse when you apply your "move over" aids just as the horse is about to lift the leg that's moving laterally—the inside hind when doing a shoulder-in for instance. Later, when you and your horse are doing half-halts, you will find that in one moment of the stride you're asking the horse to get ready to halt, but then, in the next moment, you're asking him not to halt but to continue on. When you put half-halts together with lateral movement, say in a pirouette, it begins to feel as though you're riding each footfall individually.

Aids That Release

Now I admit this is beginning to sound very complex and technical. Aids with moments of silence applied at just the right moment? How can anyone use aids with such precision? Relax. It's not very difficult at all. All of this discussion about the aids comes down to working in the horse's rhythm. When you sit correctly, relax, and create contact with your weight (see Ch. 9, *Contact*), the horse will do most of the work. When you're relaxed, the horse moves you as he moves. Riding this way, applying an aid becomes a question of slightly exaggerating or resisting that motion. That's all it takes to use aids in the rhythm of the horse.

Of course, to ride this sensitively, you must learn to use aids that release. That is, apply an aid by softening the contact first and then restoring it. For example, to ask the horse to yield to the right rein, don't just squeeze the rein. First, soften the contact in the right rein then renew it. Instead of squeezing with a leg or poking your horse with your heel for a leg aid, just lighten your leg a little and then let it rest on your horse again.

By always reducing the contact of the leg or hand in the moment before an aid is applied, the horse learns that an aid will be applied immediately after the contact has been removed for a moment. He then begins to react to the relaxation of the aids. When a horse is sensitive to relaxation of the aids, he can perform with absolutely no interference from them. There is nothing preventing him from moving freely and loosely.

Riding with aids of reason—aids that request, encourage, allow—is the ideal that we strive for.

Riding with aids of reason—aids that request, encourage and allow—is the ideal that we strive for. It is a real, attainable ideal. You need to develop a correct seat and learn how to create contact properly. Then, it's a matter of teaching the horse what the aids mean and that as their name implies, the aids are there to help him and guide him to the balance and comfort that he wants to have so that he can enjoy the experience of being ridden as much as you enjoy riding him.

7 Correctly Speaking...

When making corrections, it is important to remember we are not using aids that request, encourage, and allow, we are making a correction which should be "clear, effective and over with." (See Ch. 4, *Rule 4— Correction Not Punishment.*) Corrections are similar to aids, but they are not aids. It is an error to think or act as if they are. Corrections are meant to stop a horse from doing something wrong and show him what he should be doing instead.

Discussing ideal aids in the last chapter, I used the analogy of juggling objects. Corrections require that you drop most of these objects to concentrate on just one or two for a moment. Once you've fixed the problem, pick up everything else and begin again. The aids deal with all aspects of the horse's movement, while corrections address a specific problem.

All too often riders mistake a correction that worked, for an aid. Then, they begin to use the *correction* to make requests. They've forgotten the exercise-reward cycle—"first ask correctly, then make correct." For example, if your horse doesn't turn left in response to light aids, you may have to use strong reins. Fine, that got him to turn left once. Now the next time you ask him to turn left, you must ask him correctly with light requests, even though the light aids failed on the previous attempt and the stronger correction succeeded.

I know using what failed instead of what succeeded sounds incredibly strange! But stop for a moment and consider that in training your goal isn't just to get the horse to turn left—it's to teach him to turn left in response to the aids that request, encourage, and allow. It's only by always going back to these aids and then correcting if necessary that a horse learns what the aids mean and how he should react to them.

To continue the above example of turning left, the second time you want to turn left you'll first ask correctly with the aids. More than likely, your horse won't respond the right way this time either, so you will have to use a strong rein like before. But you almost certainly won't have to use as strong a rein or hold it for as long to get the correct result. Each time you go through the cycle of asking him to turn left and then turning him left, you'll find it takes less and less of a correction, until soon he turns in response to just your aids.

Correction Techniques

There are two basic techniques for making corrections with a horse. The first is to exaggerate an aid by slowly applying it with gradually increasing force. The second is to be abrupt—to use quick, light taps with your legs, spurs, or whip. Sometimes light slaps or tweaks with the reins are also appropriate.

Force and Corrections

When making a correction by exaggerating an aid with more force, do it slowly so the correction has a chance to affect the horse. Exaggerated aids applied in the time frame of an ideal aid, within a single stride, degenerate to jerks on the rein, or kicks. An increase in force should be a correction, not violence.

In this context, making a correction clear, effective, and over with, means you should not allow it to degenerate into a tug of war. If you hold an exaggerated aid for more than two or three strides, abandon that particular technique and find an exercise that works on the specific problem. For example, when attempting to correct a problem while working in the trot, if unsuccessful after several strides, abandon the trot and work in the walk until you solve the problem. Otherwise, the correction has turned into dull, heavy riding.

If a horse is being a little dull, using the quick, light technique of correction is often appropriate. With this technique you may give the horse several light taps with your leg or a light slap or tweak on the nose with the rein. Make these actions very lightly so as not to injure the horse or even cause him discomfort. Their effectiveness is in the speed with which you apply them, not in their force. They are merely intended to get a little more attention and, frankly, to annoy the horse just a little. With either technique, the amount of force to use is the least amount necessary to make your intentions clear. Too little and the horse will learn to ignore you—too much and he'll become afraid of you.

Knowing how much force is just the right amount of force is not complicated. To the contrary, it is something we do so normally we do it unconsciously. For example, imagine you are standing next to a small child who is about to run into traffic. You would first stop him by grabbing his arm and then explain to him about the dangers of traffic. When you grab his arm, you would use just enough force to get the job done. Not so little that he runs right by you and does not stop, but not so much you dislocate his shoulder either. Once stopped, you wouldn't go into a dissertation on the physical effects of impact on the human body by large masses traveling at high velocities. You would find words that he could understand to explain he should play in his yard and not run into traffic.

This is all that corrections are. Just enough force to stop the incorrect behavior coupled with an explanation of what is correct. I can't tell you how much force is required to correct your horse any more than I can tell you how much is required to stop the child, but I can tell you the attitude should be the same. Just as I can't tell you which words will explain traffic to the child, I can't tell you which exercise will solve a particular problem with your horse. However, you will need to find a way, when dealing with either horse or child, to make your explanations understandable so that your corrections are always clear, effective, and over with.

8 The Fine Art of Doing Nothing!

Frankly, I'm lazy. I always have been and most probably always will be. This isn't such a bad thing in riding because "the least you do, the better you are."[2] Wow! What a sport! Custom tailored to me!

Although instructors and authors are always talking about things you should do, the most important thing is to do nothing at all and do it very, very well. Before you can do anything correctly, you have to do nothing well. You must be able to just sit there and not interfere with the horse.

When you sit on a moving horse, his back moves your seat, so you have to separate your seat from your legs and back. Otherwise, you'll be accidentally kicking him, and uncontrollably jerking on the reins. This is the purpose of a correct position. Because a correct position that separates your seat is so important, a chapter on it appears here, as well as in virtually every other book on rid-

> *...the most important thing is to do nothing at all and do it very, very well.*

---

2 *The phrase, "The least you do, the better you are," is a constant mantra of Alex Konyot. Born in Hungary in 1915, and living in the U.S. since 1943, he has been a performer, trainer, and teacher of classical horsemanship his entire life. During his career he has trained more than 60 horses to do the Grand-Prix movements, and many of those to perform airs above the ground.*

ing and training. Only a position that allows an independent seat gives you control of your aids.

It's possible to feel how a correct position works from the ground. Stand as shown in figure 6 and hollow your back by moving your buttocks back and pressing your belly button forward. In this position you will notice that you can move your hips a little forward and back, left and right, up and down, and the motion is isolated between your knees and the small of your back.

If your back isn't hollowed a bit this way, you lose the independence of your seat. You can feel this from the ground too. Begin in the position shown here and straighten your back by tucking your buttocks down and forward a little. Now if you move your hips a little forward and back, left and right, you'll see that your whole body from ankles to shoulders moves with them. Because your shoulders are moving, your arms and hands are moving as well, and, if your hands move with your seat, you'll never be able to have the soft, quiet hands your horse needs.

This does not mean that I expect riders to trot about with stiff, hollow backs. Quite the contrary—if you start with this position, the motion of the horse will move it from slightly hollowed to straight and back to slightly hollow again. This gives the appearance of a straight back and quiet seat; however, your seat is moving with your horse and your back is flexing to accommodate that movement.

Once you're sitting on your seat bones, all you have to do is keep your upper body up, and let gravity do the rest. That's it. Sit up straight and let everything else fall.

When viewed from the side there should be an imaginary line perpendicular to the ground through your ears, shoulders, hips, and ankles. To maintain this position, however, the saddle has to help.

A Seat You Can Buy!

To a large extent, a good position and a correct seat are purchased. Before you can sit up straight and be comfortable, you need a comfortable seat that is parallel to the ground. Many saddles do not provide this. If a saddle does not have a good, level seat, you're not going to have a good, balanced seat. You will always be fighting gravity and rounding your back, sitting on your buttocks instead of your seat bones.

Looking at a good saddle from the side, the panels should place even pressure along their length on the horse's back. The pommel should slope down to the actual seat of the saddle, the place where we sit. The seat has a slight curve but is effectively flat, and it should be in the middle of the saddle (fig. 7).

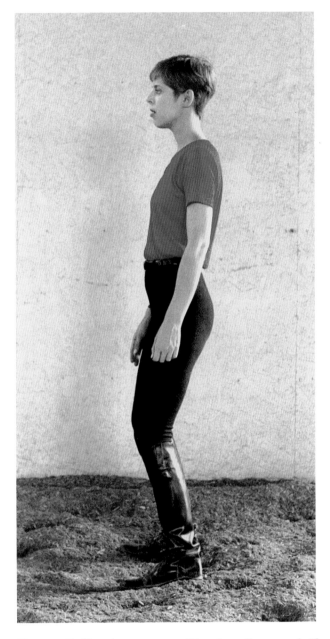

Figure 6 Feeling the correct position from the ground. If you stand with your back hollow, your belly button forward, and move your hips, you will notice the motion is isolated between your knees and the small of your back. This is the basis of an independent seat.

Figure 7 To sit correctly, you need a good saddle like the one in this photo. The arrows show the area where you sit, which must be almost flat, and parallel to the ground.

Women are wider in the pelvis than men and therefore need wider saddles, but they also need a level seat to sit on.

A correct saddle makes finding a correct seat a simple matter. If you drop your stirrups, sit up straight, and walk around on a loose rein for a few minutes, your seat will find you. Within several minutes you will be sitting in the deepest part of the saddle on your seat bones, and that is all that you need. To develop this seat as a matter of habit, walk around without stirrups regularly.

Your legs should just rest on the horse. If you relax them, gravity is enough to keep them quiet. If you grip, your muscles will be tense and you

How to Check You Are Sitting Straight (*Figures 8, 9, 10*)

Figure 8 **When you let your arm fall, your elbow should rest at your midline.**

won't feel your horse. If your legs are moving uncontrollably, the horse won't know when you are making a request or when you are just bouncing.

Sometimes people find it difficult to know when they're leaning forward, leaning back, or sitting up straight. Here's a simple check. Put both reins in one hand and let your other arm drop. If your elbow rests on your midline, you're sitting straight (fig. 8). If your elbow hangs in front of you, you're leaning forward (fig. 9). If your elbow hangs behind you, you're leaning back (fig. 10).

Figure 9 You are leaning forward if your elbow hangs in front of your midline.

To lighten your seat, rock ever so slightly forward onto the front of your seat bones, putting more weight on them but not so much as to lift the rear of your bones from the saddle. It may be difficult to realize how small a shift this is while in the saddle; however, the subtlety of this aid may be felt by sitting straight in a hard chair and then rocking onto your forward seat bones. It is a very small amount.

To brace your back, stay upright, push your belly button out and open your chest by trying to make your shoulder blades touch. To sit in the deepest, strongest position, brace your back and put a little more weight on your rear seat bones—again not so much that you lift your front bones from the saddle.

Figure 10 *You are slouching back (behind the vertical) if your elbow rests behind your midline.*

Your head should be up and you should be looking where you are going. When turning or doing lateral work, keep your head straight and turn your whole upper body from the waist. This points your belly button in the direction you are going and shifts your weight just enough to be a weight aid—a very subtle aid, but seat aids should be subtle.

The actual position of your arms and hands isn't as important as the way you position them. Relaxing your shoulders and elbows so your hands fall into place is more than related to contact—it's the source of *contact*.

9 Contact

By far the most perplexing questions in riding deal with *contact:* what it is, what it does, how to get it, and what to do with it when you have it. These need to be addressed because the absence of correct contact is going to ruin just about every other aspect of your riding. You may have the best timing, horse, equipment, attitude, and theories available, but without correct contact, they will never amount to much. Conversely, with correct contact you can cut a lot of other corners and still have very credible results. Contact is really that important.

Contact is the physical connection between horse and rider. It is the horse and rider touching each other. When you turn a page of this book, you are in "contact" with the page as you turn it. When you shake hands upon meeting someone, you are in contact with him.

Contact allows you to feel your horse and your horse to feel you. It's the small changes in how you feel to the horse that let him know what you're asking. The small changes in

You may have the best timing, horse, equipment, attitude, and theories available, but without correct contact, they will never amount to much.

how the horse feels to you are how you know if the horse is performing as you wish. Now you can see why having correct contact is so important, and why not having correct contact is such a big problem. Contact is what we ride with.

In fact, with correct contact, you can feel the horse about to fall out of balance, or change his direction. When you feel these before they actually occur, you can help him keep his balance and direction with your aids while "juggling" the rest of his movement—gait, direction, angle, frame, bend, tempo, stride, and energy. If, on the other hand, you don't help your horse before he actually loses his balance or changes his direction, you will probably have to use some form of correction.

Feelings end where tension begins, and to ride without tension you not only need a correct position, you must have obtained the position the right way.

It's possible to feel a horse getting ready to change because even a small horse is pretty big, and it takes a fair amount of effort on his part to change movement, direction, or speed. As a result, he has to shift his weight and use muscles differently before he can make a change. Riding with correct contact, you can feel these shifts in weight and muscle. You can feel him moving against your leg before he throws his quarters in or out. You can feel a horse start to go more into the bridle before he stiffens and falls in or out. When you feel these changes about to happen, there is a moment before the horse is committed to the shift in weight to lightly use your rein or leg and say, "No, stay here with me please."

The Importance of a Correct Position

Feeling ends where tension begins, and to ride without tension you not only need a correct position, you must have obtained the position the right way. When sitting as explained in the last chapter, you sit on your seat bones and rest your legs on the horse. Sitting this way lets you feel your horse through your seat and legs.

To have correct contact through the reins, your upper arms should remain almost perpendicular to the ground. This places the elbows near the midpoint of the body when viewed from the side, and relieves the shoulders of the weight of the upper arm. The shoulder and back muscles, therefore, remain soft and relaxed. Ideally, the forearms should be positioned to create a straight line from bit to elbow. Your wrists should remain straight, but relaxed.

Figure 11 The snaffle rein should come from the bit through your third and fourth fingers, and out between your first finger and thumb. Hold the rein as close to your palm as possible so you can keep it from slipping through your fingers with the least amount of tension in your hand.

The snaffle rein should come from the bit through your third and fourth fingers and out between your first finger and thumb (fig. 11). Hold the rein as close to the palm as possible so you can keep it from slipping through your fingers with the least amount of tension in your hand. To find just how little tension is required, squeeze your hand into a fist as tightly as possible and hold it until you can feel the tension in your wrist and forearm, and then your elbow and shoulder. Now relax your hand until you feel the tension in your shoulder, elbow, forearm, and wrist go away. This is the correct force to close your hands on the reins—just below the point where it becomes tension that travels up your arm.

When your arms are in this relaxed position, your elbows and shoulders remain flexible, and you can feel your horse through the reins. However, many riders have the right position for the wrong reason. Rather than allowing their arms to fall into the correct position by relaxing their muscles so that their hands are soft and still, they try to hold this position by tensing their muscles and their hands become stiff. This simply doesn't work. For contact to be useful you have to relax your muscles so your arm can just fall into the right position.

It's altogether likely that you have already heard or read that you should imagine weights in your elbows, springs in your arms, or pulleys over your shoulders to visualize correct contact. You don't have to. In fact, there are weights on your elbows, springs in your arms, and pulleys over your shoulders in reality. So, you don't need to imagine them, you do need to feel them. I could go through a long explanation of how gravity, biomechanics, and vector forces create the weights, springs, and pulleys needed for contact, but about halfway through the third sentence of that explanation, you'd put this book down and never pick it up again. So I'm just going to give you a few simple exercises to help you feel how just letting your arms fall creates proper contact.

Contact Exercise Number One

When doing these exercises it helps if you stand with your back slightly hollow as described in the previous chapter (p. 54). Begin by bringing the fingers of one arm up and let them rest on your shoulder as shown in figure 12A. Next, allow your elbow to fall into the position shown in figure 12B in a smooth fluid motion. Continue to bring your elbow up and let it down until you can feel the tension in your shoulder increase as you raise your elbow and decrease as you let your elbow come down and just hang.

Contact Exercise Number Two

For the rest of these exercises close your hand and keep your wrists straight as though holding the reins, so you can begin to get a sense of what it is like to ride with elbows and shoulders so loose that your hand just falls into place. The second exercise begins with your elbow up and forward and your forearm held vertically as shown in figure 13A. Now, as you let your elbow fall, your forearm goes from vertical to horizontal as in figure 13B. Repeat this

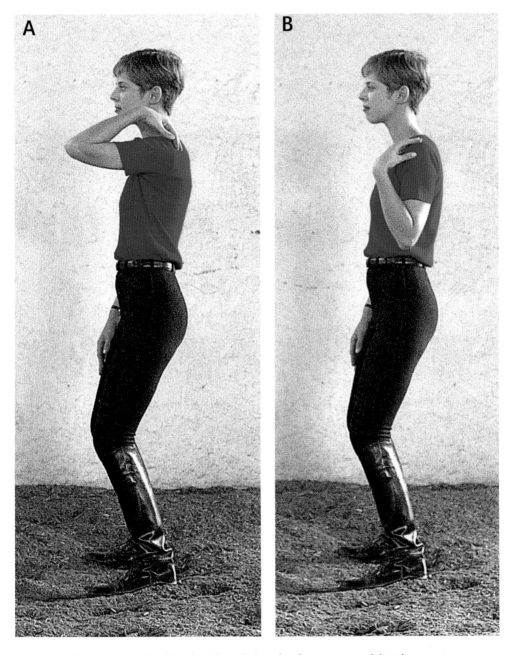

Figure 12 Contact Exercise Number One: *Bring the fingers up and let them rest on your shoulder. Next, allow the elbow to fall into the position shown. This first exercise is used to isolate and relax the muscles in your shoulders.*

Figure 13 **Contact Exercise Number Two:** *Begin with your elbow up and forward and let your arm fall. Continue the exercise until you feel your shoulder free up and fall naturally in the position shown.*

exercise until you feel how your arm just "falls" into this position and keeping it there is effortless.

Contact Exercise Number Three

The purpose of the previous two exercises was to release tension from your shoulder and give you the feeling of letting your arm fall into the position shown in figure 14B. This exercise is designed to relax your elbow and give you the feeling of it bending as it falls into position.

Begin with your forearm forward about 45 degrees as depicted in figure 14A. Now as you bring your arm to position, feel your elbow closing as it moves down and back. As you move it forward and up again, feel your elbow opening. Repeat this exercise until you can move your arm back and forth from the position shown in figure 14A to figure 14B, in a smooth, fluid, steady motion.

Contact Exercise Number Four

Once you have this feeling of being free in your shoulder and elbow in both arms, it's time to get the feeling of "releasing the horse" by giving the reins. In this exercise, push your elbow forward while keeping your forearm horizontal and then let it fall back into position again. This exercise is shown in figure 15A and B.

Notice in figure 15B, that when your muscles are relaxed and your elbow bends freely, your upper arm falls a little behind the vertical. This simple fact, that our arms will fall behind the vertical when our elbows are bent and muscles relaxed, is the source of correct contact. Because our arms fall behind the vertical, we can simply adjust the reins so that they, the reins, hold our arms, at or slightly in front of, the vertical. In this way, contact is determined by a very small percentage of the weight of our arms. Since there is no tension in our elbows or shoulders, the contact is soft and fluid.

To ride with a heavier contact, simply shorten your reins a little. This brings your arms further forward, so more of their weight quite literally makes the contact heavier. Yet your muscles will still be relaxed, and the contact remains soft and fluid.

Higher Hands For a While

By keeping your forearms horizontal for a while it will be easier to get the feeling of creating contact through the weight of your arms, and it will help you to stay loose in your elbows and shoulders. If you keep your elbows close to your hips you'll also begin to understand how your reins and seat can work together. It will feel as though your rein aids go through your seat, and

Figure 14 Contact Exercise Number Three: With your hand closed as though holding a rein, raise your arm with your upper arm parallel to the ground and your forearm at a 45-degree angle. Feel your elbow opening as you do this, and closing as it falls back to your side.

Figure 15 Contact Exercise Number Four: *Keeping your forearm horizontal, push your elbow forward and let it gently fall back into position.*

Figure 16 **This photo demonstrates how to correctly shorten your left rein.**

you will have the sensation of molding the horse with your hands, seat, and legs. Once you are comfortable with this feeling you can let your forearms fall into a position that creates a straight line from bit to elbow.

Adjusting the Reins

Of course, to adjust contact by setting rein length, you have to be able to adjust the reins correctly. This is fairly simple, as only two adjustments ever need to be made to the reins: they get either longer or shorter. To make a rein longer, relax your fingers and let it slip through your hand to the proper length. It is just that simple. To make a rein shorter, grab the rein just above your other hand and pull it.

Using the specific example of shortening the left rein, (see fig. 16) the procedure is:

1. Grasp the left rein just above the left thumb with your right thumb and forefinger.
2. Relax your left hand and pull the left rein through about an inch or so, a little up and back toward your chest. (As you do this, sit up a little straighter as a reminder not to slouch.)
3. Release the left rein and let your right hand and arm fall back into position.

If you learn nothing else in your entire riding career, learn to relax, sit quietly, and have soft contact.

If you need to adjust more than the inch or so, do it several times. To shorten both reins, shorten one, then the other. Any other method is going to make you reach forward for a rein, which brings your shoulders forward and seat out of the saddle.

These simple techniques for adjusting the reins are the last of the techniques I have for teaching students how to ride with quiet, soft, relaxed contact. This ability, or lack of it, affects every aspect of your riding. If you can't be soft and relaxed on top of your horse, your horse will never be soft and relaxed under you. If you learn nothing else in your entire riding career, learn to relax, sit quietly, and have soft contact.

10 Rein Effects

Rein effects are really used for green horses. As the horse develops, the use of the reins becomes much more subtle and it appears as though the rider is not moving his hands or using the reins at all. Indeed, when riders refer to using just their fingers to manipulate the reins, they are speaking of the ideal and when your horse is trained you shouldn't need any more effort than just that.

However, trying to ride with only your fingers early on won't work. A green horse won't have a clue about what you want. So if you start working your fingers open and shut, the horse will ignore you, then you'll do it some more and pretty soon start to get tense in your hand, wrist, forearm, elbow, and shoulders. Then it's all over—you and your horse, are both tight and tense.

To get to the point where the reins can be used in such a subtle way, the manner in which they are applied in early training is what counts. You need to keep your elbows close to your body while using them. Then immediately go back to just the soft contact that comes from allowing your hands to fall into place as described in the last chapter.

I recommend five rein effects: *direct, open, half release, hitchhiker,* and the *just-plain-stop.* For purposes of description, each is defined separately, yet in actual practice it is common for them to be used in combination.

The *direct rein* is really more a seat aid than a rein aid. The outside hand does hold the rein and accept the energy, but it's the seat—more particularly the outside hip—pressing slightly forward toward the hand, that creates the effect. By this definition you can see that the direct rein is a very subtle aid, and as it works on the bars of the mouth, it has to be. In addition, since it is a proper aid and not a correction, it has to be applied and released within a single stride.

There are times in riding when it's better to stop the horse, reorganize, and try again, than to attempt to fix the problems while still moving.

The *opening rein* is widely used in all riding disciplines. While usually used as an inside rein aid, there are times when the outside rein will be opened a little as well. To apply the opening rein, the hand is taken away from the horse. When riding on a circle, the inside hand is taken toward the center of the circle. In addition, the hand is rotated in proportion to the degree the rein is opened, so that the thumb is pointed a little away from the horse. The technique of rotating the hand in this fashion allows the rider to keep his elbow near his hip and encourages the correct proportion of seat and leg in support of it. The opening rein is always an invitation. Any attempt to use this rein aid with strength will tend to pull the rider off balance.

The *half release* (fig. 17A and B) is actually in common use. It just doesn't have a name. So I'm coining this name (I think), which comes in part from the *crest release* used in jumping. This rein aid is much less obvious than a crest release and, as the horse's training progresses it should end up being invisible. With the half release the hand is brought a little up and a little forward. The amount of contact should not vary, just the direction of it. Viewed from the side, one can imagine the bit as the hub of a wheel, the rein as a spoke, and the hand as a point on the rim rolling the wheel forward.

For the half release (fig.18) to be effective, the horse must be properly prepared from the ground. In particular, he must have been taught to yield to upward contact by softening in his jaw, poll, and neck. The horse is taught this response by use of exercises called *flexions*, which are discussed in Ch.18, *Soften, Bend, and Move Into the Hand*.

The last of these useful effects I call the *hitchhiker rein* (fig.19). This rein effect is a correction, not an aid. It is used out of rhythm for more than the length of time of one stride. It has a definite mechanical effect in that it will

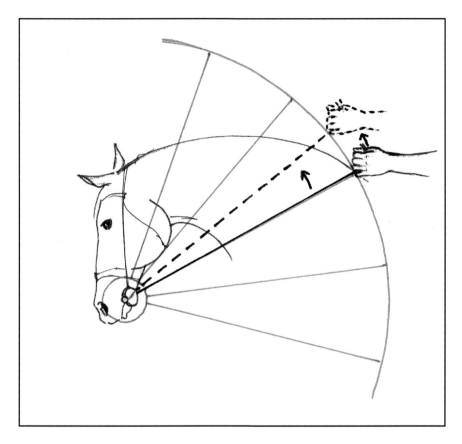

Figure 17 With the half-release rein effect, the hand is brought a little up and forward. Viewed from the side, one can imagine the bit as the hub of a wheel, the rein as a spoke, and the rider's hand on the rim rolling the wheel forward.

bring the horse's head off to the side. Like the half release, the horse must first be prepared with groundwork before using it, and even then, it should be used sparingly.

With the hitchhiker rein, the hand is brought up and out as though "hitch-hiking" for a ride on the side of the road. Its directional components are up and out, away from the horse. It is very important that the rider's elbows stay close to the body so that the seat and leg are automatically brought into play.

Figure 18 **Half-release contact: Karen shows how the contact remains the same when she brings her hand up and forward.**

The purpose of this effect is twofold. First, in any situation where the horse is being rather enthusiastically disobedient, it may be used to bring the horse's nose to the rider's knee. A horse that is over bent is in no position to rear, buck, or bolt. When used in this situation, a rider can feel free to exag-

Figure 19 *When using the hitchhiker rein, the hand is brought up and out, as though you are hitchhiking a ride from the side of the road. It is very important that the rider's elbow stays close to her body, so that her seat and leg automatically help make clear her request to move over.*

gerate his seat and press his belly button more forward while bringing his shoulders well behind the vertical. This is absolutely the best and safest way to sit through or discourage out-and-out rebellion. As the pressure of the bit is still directed to the corners rather than the bars, and the object is to prevent violence on the part of the horse instead of meeting it with violence on the part of the rider, it is the preferred method of dealing with this type of situation as it complies with the five rules previously outlined.

The other and more common use of the hitchhiker rein is to sensitize the horse to the request to displace his shoulder to the outside of his bend. Using this rein effect more conservatively with a slight exaggeration of the back and seat helps the horse to understand that he should soften to the inside rein, bend from the inside leg, and step into the outside hand (fig. 19). While it is absolutely valid to use this rein effect in training, it should be considered a training-correction device and be replaced with the less coercive half release as early on as possible. The method for making the transition from hitchhiker to half release is to always use the half release first. If the horse responds to that, success! If not, simply maintain the contact and change the direction of the aid until it is a hitchhiker rein.

The *Just-Plain-Stop* Rein

There are times in riding when it's better to just stop the horse, reorganize, and try again, than to attempt to fix the problems while still moving. The method I've found that offers the most effect with the least coercion I call the *just-plain-stop* rein.

The *just-plain-stop* (fig. 20) uses both reins at the same time. To apply it, the rider should first brace his back by pushing his belly button and chest out while bringing the shoulders back and raise his hands up toward the center of his chest. The use of this combination makes it so uncomfortable for the horse to move, it is an effective mechanical means of stopping or slowing him.

The fact that it is very uncomfortable for the horse makes it important that we do not use it too often or too strongly. Because it is so mechanically effective, it is not necessary to use much force with the hands. Just bringing the hands up with normal contact and a braced back will usually do the job. Rather than increase the force on the reins, leaning back a bit further behind the vertical has a much stronger effect. Of course that effect is directed toward the horse's back, so to avoid making the horse sore, use it as little and as mildly as possible.

On the plus side, it will stop or slow just about any horse except for a panic-stricken runaway. Also, if the rider first braces his back, then waits a

Figure 20 The just-plain-stop *rein effect uses both reins at the same time. The rider braces her back and is raising her hands up toward the center of her chest. Just bringing the hands up with normal contact and a braced back will usually do the job. Rather than just increasing the force on the reins, leaning back a bit further behind the vertical has a much stronger effect.*

moment before bringing his hands up, the horse will soon become sensitive to the action of the rider's seat and back and will begin to slow down before the hands are raised. (This is exactly the same psychological principle as the dog "sitting" before the trainer lifts his head, which I mentioned in Chapter 2.) This is useful because when performed subtly, the just-plain-stop rein effect is similar to the aids for a half-halt.

The simplest way to avoid using too much force with this rein effect, is to be sure and soften both reins at least once per stride. The horse will need to have his head for a moment to be able to stop. Try it and you'll find the horse always stops at the moment the reins are released, not when the reins are taken up.

The Indirect Rein

There is one other rein effect that is in such common use it seems no book about riding is published without giving some mention of it—the *indirect rein*. This effect is brought about by bringing the inside hand toward the wither and pulling on it. A *terrible* thing to do! The theory of its proponents is that it bends the horse and prevents him from falling in. In fact, it may coerce the horse into bending his neck, but it prevents the horse stretching the outside rib cage and bending correctly. Instead, it compresses the inside rib cage and prohibits an even bend from poll to dock. The compression of the inside rib cage prevents the horse from bringing his inside hind leg up and under him, eliminating the possibility of proper development of the quarters. By now you have determined that I don't favor this rein effect at all and are probably wondering why I bothered to mention it at all. Well, it's because my publisher told me I had to!

11

Reiny Daze

By default, if you're training a horse, you're changing him. This means as he changes, you will have to ride him differently than you did before. For some reason, discussions about how to change the way you use the reins when going from a green to an advanced horse are virtually non-existent. This has led to terrible confusion. Countless riders are trying to ride advanced horses with rein techniques only suitable for green horses, while many others try to ride green horses with techniques only suitable for advanced horses. This chapter is meant to clarify the differences and to offer some guides to help you use the reins on green horses so that they can become advanced horses.

Countless riders are trying to ride advanced horses with rein techniques only suitable for green horses, while many others try to ride green horses with techniques only suitable for advanced horses.

Whether you're riding a green or fully trained horse, you absolutely must have the ability to ride with the passive, completely relaxed contact described in Chapter 9. The contact developed from just the weight of your arms with completely relaxed muscles is your starting point. Rein aids are developed by varying this contact, so if you don't have this to begin with, you can't use proper rein aids.

There are three ways in which you can alter your basic contact. You can increase it, decrease it, or change the direction of it. With the advanced horse, these variations are barely perceptible changes in fingers or flicks of the wrist. These light little touches and variations have no mechanical effect and rely on the horse's knowledge and willingness for their effectiveness. With green horses, rein aids are created with movements involving your whole arm and seat. The bigger aids (rein effects) make it clear to the green horse what you want. They also have a limited mechanical effect.

Even the larger movements of your hand can be used as aids that request, encourage, and allow, or as corrections that are "clear, effective, and over with". When used as an aid, the rein effect is made by merely moving your hand, so the direction of the rein changes while the contact remains steady, or is made lighter. If this doesn't have the result you want, then you have the option of gradually increasing the contact to be more persuasive.

Aids That Release

Most often, you should use your rein by simply softening or *releasing* one rein or the other. To release the rein, just push your elbow a little forward to soften the contact, and then let it fall back into position. If you move your elbow forward and let it fall back in a soft, fluid manner, you have released the rein.

If you're on a horse that wants to lean on the reins, the reins should always have that "wobbly" feel to them.

If you feel a horse beginning to fall out of balance and lean on a rein, simply release the rein by bringing your elbow forward until the contact is softened or dropped, and the horse will re-balance himself. This is similar in concept to leaning on a fence post. If the post has a nice secure, solid feel to it, you might lean on it. If the post feels wobbly, as though it's going to fall down under the slightest provocation, you won't lean on it. If you started to lean on it and felt it start to give under your weight, you would stop leaning and stand up straight again so that you didn't fall down.

If you're on a horse that wants to lean on the reins, the reins should always have that "wobbly" feel to them.

Consistent Contact, Pulling, and Stretching

When riding a green horse trying to keep his balance by leaning on the reins, you're going to have to release the reins a lot. During this period, you will have to keep guiding him back to the correct frame and then releasing him again. It's the only way the horse will learn to find his own balance and not rely on the reins.

While the young horse is trying to lean on the reins for support, the inside rein should be released fairly often—perhaps as much as every other stride. The outside rein will have to be softened occasionally too, although not as often and generally not as much as the inside rein. All of this releasing and giving of the reins makes it appear as though you are just a bit sloppy, a little too loose, or too free. However, if you just keep the horse soft, after a while he'll learn to stay in balance while carrying you, and then he'll remain in a fairly consistent frame. As he becomes steady, so should you. The more accomplished the horse is at staying soft and in balance, the less you should be doing.

...contact is not simply a question of having a single contact that is applicable in all situations.

Once a horse has learned to balance himself without leaning on the reins, he will begin to figure out that he can reach out to the reins and stretch his back. Most horses, especially long-backed horses, will need to spend some time in a frame that is longer and lower than ideal so their muscles have a chance to strengthen as their topline develops. During this period of stretching and developing muscles, you will usually have to allow the horse to take a heavier contact or feel of the reins.

Allowing the horse a heavier contact while he is stretching isn't at odds with releasing the rein when he is leaning or pulling. A horse needs to stretch to develop his muscles correctly, and he needs you to stop him from pulling so he can learn to balance himself. What you need to know is the difference between stretching and pulling.

When a horse is stretching he will stay bent throughout his body and he will still soften to your rein aids. His tempo will remain steady, and although the contact may be a bit heavy, it will still feel soft. A horse that is pulling will lose his bend and stiffen in his body. As you use the reins, he'll get stiffer and pull harder. His tempo will get quicker and his strides shorter as he goes.

You can see that contact is not simply a question of having a single contact that is applicable in all situations. There are times when having almost no contact is correct for a horse; there are times when a little too much contact is correct for a horse. Eventually though, your horse will learn to balance himself and then develop the muscles he needs to carry you. As he does, he won't need to stretch as much, and his head and neck will begin to elevate. When this happens, the contact will be fairly steady and comfortably light.

When the horse begins to accept a light, steady contact while remaining in a frame consistently, you will still have to release the contact from time to time to remind him to stay soft and in balance. At this stage, the release won't be as obvious as when he was learning to balance himself. Instead of dropping the contact completely, just soften it a little. Once the horse understands the reins are there only for guidance, not for support, the roles will begin to change. A fully trained horse seeks the light touch of the reins, as though to say, "Are you there? Is this correct? Am I doing it right?" and upon receiving this assurance, will drop the contact the slightest amount.

A fully trained horse seeks the light touch of the reins, as though to say, "Are you there? Is this correct? Am I doing it right?"

A Few Rein Rules

To get to this ideal horse, there are a few general rules that apply to any use of the reins. They are brief and simple, and they affect every aspect of rider technique. Developing the habit of following these rules is as basic and necessary as the ability to post or sit.

Always give before you take. A rein aid should always be preceded with a softening of the rein before it is applied. The amount of contact should be reduced a degree, even if it's soft (as it should be) already. Releasing the rein before using it avoids the commonly seen tug-of-war between horse and rider.

Never drop either hand below the withers. If the hand is brought below the height of the withers, the rider's shoulder will drop, his back will round, and his seat will be taken out of the saddle to a degree. Now, rather than the hand, seat, and leg working together, the hand is just pulling on the mouth with no support or context offered by the seat and leg. Worse yet, it will by default violate the next rule.

Do not pull on the bars of the mouth. The bars are the part of the lower gum between the front teeth and rear molars that the bit touches.They have no elasticity. They are fairly hard and unyielding. Similar in consistency and sensitivity to the front of a human shinbone, they are unprotected and susceptible to painful injury. Once the bars are destroyed (a very high percentage of racehorses come off the track with deformed bars), that's it. They're beyond repair and will never be quite the same.

The corners of the mouth are almost the exact opposite. Fleshy and rub-bery, they have a lot of give and are much less prone to injury—but they can still be injured. Directing correction techniques toward the corners tends to avoid injury; however, the rider still must use technique. Please don't get the impression I'm saying it's okay to use violence on the corners. As I stated before when correcting a horse with increasing pressure it must be done slow-ly and gradually so the horse is not injured.

So how much contact is acceptable and where should an aid be directed? When it comes to the bars, the contact should just be a light touch. A rein aid directed to the bars consists of a slight release followed by touching again. It feels very much like tapping a finger lightly on a table. If the horse attempts to lean on the hands, the hands have to yield and give that "wobbly" feeling described above. If a correction needs to be made, it should be directed in an upward fashion, toward the corners of the mouth, so as to prevent any undo stress on the bars.

Never bring the inside hand across the withers. This is another way of saying to not use the indirect rein in its several varieties. As previously explained, bringing the inside hand toward the wither may bend the horse at the withers, but it actually prevents an equal bend from poll to dock. Rather than stretching the outside of the horse, it compresses the inside, which pre-vents the inside hind from engaging. Since a basis of correct training is engagement of the hind legs, the indirect rein has no place in it.

PART THREE

That Delicate Balance!

12 Developing Working Gaits

The term "working gait" describes a horse moving with his weight evenly distributed on all four feet, swinging his legs freely in long, even, ground-covering strides. He is stretched over his topline and his hind legs are well engaged. Any horse moving like this is in a working gait; it may be a walk, trot, or canter, but it's still a working gait.

Horses have a natural tendency to go *on the forehand* and put more weight on their front feet than their back feet because they support the weight of their heads and necks with their front legs. Moving on their own without a rider, that's fine; they compensate and get along quite nicely. However, the additional weight on their back increases the tendency to be on the forehand, and most horses do not compensate for this correctly.

A horse can be on the forehand because he's simply out of balance and quite literally putting one foot in front of the other to avoid falling down completely, or because he's been deliberately stretched out to develop his muscles generally, and his topline in particular.

When a horse is simply falling on his forehand, his weight is out of balance and his *movement* is out of balance as well. He doesn't use his energy efficiently and he is not building the muscles necessary to get him off his forehand.

Figure 21 Joe, a Quarter Horse, is still on his forehand at this stage of his training. Because his movement is balanced enough so that he can swing his legs freely
and engage his hocks, he will continue to develop his topline, which is still visibly lacking muscle development behind the saddle.

When a rider is stretching a horse out on his forehand, the horse still has
more weight on his forelegs than hind, but his *movement* is balanced (fig. 21).
By balancing a horse's movement while he is on his forehand, you teach him
to use his energy efficiently and build the muscles he needs to get off of his
forehand. This section explains how to balance a horse's movement so that
you can develop his strength, coordination, and understanding enough to
balance his weight.

Preparation for Developing Working Gaits

Every horse needs to learn how to balance his movement while stretching onto his forehand. Even horses with the conformation and natural ability to offer good working gaits naturally should be taught how to stretch out and balance their movement. The reason why we see so many talented youngsters fall so short of their promise is that they were never taught this skill. Balancing movement is the only way to develop a horse's topline, and the best way to loosen and warm up daily.

A horse that does not understand how to balance his movement as well as his weight cannot adjust his stride correctly and will never be able to be consistently ridden to his "spot" before a fence or stand up to the rigors of advanced dressage.

Of course, our ultimate goal is to have a horse balanced in movement and weight, but we have to begin with balancing movement. This is because the only way to get a horse to put less weight on his forelegs is to get him to put more on his rear legs. We ask a horse to take more weight on his hind legs (*engage* them), by encouraging him to bring his hind legs further under him with each stride. As the hind legs take more weight, the forehand gets lighter.

Balanced Movement and Half-Halts

Before proceeding, I have to stop for a moment and answer the question that I know many readers are asking, "Why not just do a half-halt to shift your horse's weight?" The answer is quite simple—green horses cannot do half-halts.

Asking a horse to half-halt that doesn't yet know how to half-halt, or have the strength and coordination to half-halt, is pure folly.

Asking a horse to half-halt that doesn't yet know how to half-halt, or have the strength and coordination to half-halt, is pure folly. If you try to force or coerce engagement by using your legs more strongly, most young horses will simply go faster with shorter, choppier steps and will, in fact, become less, not more, engaged. If you try to shift his weight by lifting a horse off his forehand with the reins, invariably the horse ends up dropping his back, which prevents him from doing exactly what you are asking him to do, engage. Using seat aids to ask the green horse to half-halt are at best ignored. More often the poor youngster gets thrown out of balance or confused, either of which makes him tense, and again, engagement is discouraged.

That most young horses respond to aids for half-halts incorrectly is a fact that even casual observation bears out: go to any horse show—dressage or jumping—and look at the astonishingly low percentage of horses that really do engage and move freely. Almost none. A green horse moving on his forehand doesn't have the strength or coordination to half-halt—he doesn't even know it's an option.

By contrast, a well-trained horse will be strong enough, coordinated enough, and clever enough to put more weight on his hind legs, whenever the situation calls for it. But first, we have to prepare his body and teach him how. I describe and explain how to train half-halts in Chapter 22.

When dealing with the green horse, we have to deal with balancing his motion. I admit this approach is more complex to think about than others, but it does have one advantage—this works!

13
True Balance

A horse whose movement is balanced is moving in what I call *true balance*. A horse can move in true balance when he has more weight on his forelegs than hind (on his forehand), when his weight is evenly distributed (working gaits), or when he has more weight on his hind legs than forelegs (collected gaits).

A horse is in true balance when his speed, tempo, stride, and energy are in the correct ratio to one another. In the next chapter, we'll look at how direction, bend, and angle can be used to attain true balance, but first, an explanation of what the correct ratios are.

Tempo, Stride, and Speed

Tempo is the number of hoof beats per minute. *Length of stride* is the length of each step. Tempo and stride have to be balanced with overall *speed* because tempo and stride deal with how a horse's *legs* are moving, and overall speed deals with how his *body* is moving. It seems strange to think of legs and body separately, but a body moves steadily forward like an object rolling along, while legs swing back and forth like pendulums.

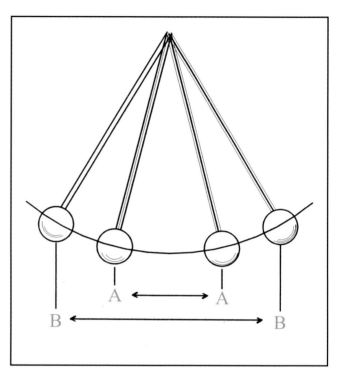

Figure 22 A pendulum travels the arc marked A–A in the same time it takes to travel the longer arc B–B. The pendulum will travel faster as it adjusts to travel the longer distance in its "natural tempo," so the motion always appears smooth and steady.

When a horse is moving in true balance, his legs swing through each stride in their natural tempo like pendulums swinging through their arcs.

A pendulum swinging back and forth accelerates to full speed, comes to a complete halt, reverses, and accelerates to full speed again so smoothly it gives the impression of constant steady motion. This same smooth motion can be seen in the legs of a horse moving in true balance.

The time it takes the pendulum to make one swing through an arc is always the same (fig. 22). If more energy is added, the pendulum will make a larger arc in the same time it takes to make the smaller arc. The pendulum travels further and faster as it adjusts its speed to travel the longer distance in its *natural tempo*.[3]

Regardless of the size of the arc or the speed of the pendulum, the tempo remains constant and the halts and reverses appear smooth. Anything that interferes with the motion of the pendulum alters its natural tempo and disrupts the smoothness.

---

3 *To be technical, the time a pendulum takes to make one pass through an arc is known as its period. However, pendulums are not usually connected in series nor is their pivot point attached to a moving body. So, in this context the phrase "natural tempo" seems more appropriate.*

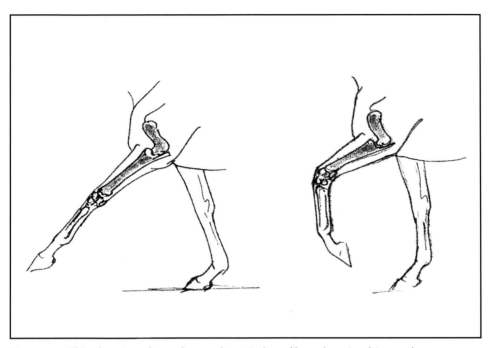

Figure 23 This drawing shows how a horse's legs (front legs in this case) can swing in extension, and in collection.

Natural Tempo and Energy

A horse's front leg can be visualized as a series of pendulums: forearm, cannon, pastern, and lower pastern. Individually each has the ability to swing smoothly within its range of motion, and they can work together to have the quality of smooth, uninterrupted motion in a wide range of arcs.

As shown in figure 23, a horse can open the arc of his front legs and reach by straightening his knee as it swings forward, or he can keep his knee bent and move with a higher rounded step. Although these are two very different strides, they are both swinging, and each has the potential to do so smoothly, in the horse's natural tempo.

When legs swing in their natural tempo, the motion is smooth, and the body appears to be rolling over them. However, if the speed, tempo, stride, and energy are not balanced, the motion looks rough and jerky.

The horse's hind legs may also be thought of as a series of pendulums with all the qualities of the front legs just described. In addition, they are attached to the hips so that when the horse is moving correctly, his back can act like a leaf spring to receive energy from, and add energy to, the hind legs (fig. 24). When a horse uses his back this way, the motion of his back is part of his stride. It appears to be round, swinging, undulating, and elastic. Yes, all these terms describe the same thing—the horse using his back properly. Often, when horses use their backs correctly, riders will say their horses are "connected" or "through." Of course, it does feel as though the energy is coming "through" the horse, and it should, because that is exactly what is happening.

In order for a horse to use his back correctly, it must be relaxed so that it can accept and return energy, and there must be enough energy for him to accept and return. Too little, and the back isn't used at all—too much and it becomes tense.

The most obvious example of a horse using his back to the utmost is the galloping race horse. As his hind legs come forward under him, they appear to be pulling his spine with them each stride. In fact, the legs are putting energy into the back much in the same way that energy is transferred into an elastic band when it is stretched. The result is that the back arches up as the hind legs come forward, and as the legs hit the ground and begin their rearward thrust, they not only use their own energy but the energy returned from the back as well.

The horse that best used his back and the natural swing of his legs at speed was Secretariat. While winning the final leg of the Triple Crown at Belmont by 30 lengths and setting the record for a mile-and-a-half distance that still stands today, he looked as though he was out for a Sunday canter through the park. He just let his legs swing out and carry him forward.

Perhaps the finest example of a horse that used natural tempo and swung his legs freely throughout the whole range of gaits is Rembrandt. He was ridden to two, consecutive Dressage World Championships, and two, consecutive individual Olympic Gold medals (Seoul '88 and Barcelona '92), by his owner Nicole Uphoff Becker. Because he always moved his legs like pendulums, always swinging them freely, he maintained the same tempo from piaffe to extension, and from gait to gait. The rhythm of his walk was four-beat, his trot two-beat, and his canter three-beat, but the tempo remained constant.

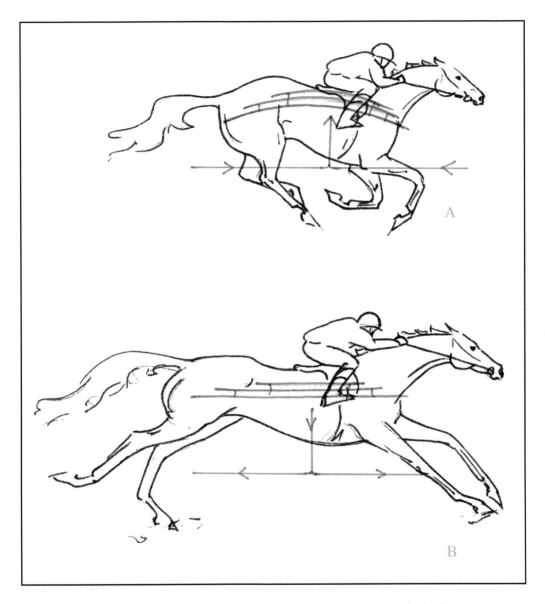

Figure 24 As the horse's hind legs come forward, they store energy in the back, which acts like a leaf spring raising up as it accepts the energy (A). As the legs hit the ground and push the horse forward, the process is reversed and the horse's back presses down, returning energy back to the legs (B).

14 Direction, Angle, and Bend

Now we can see that a horse in true balance swings his legs freely in their natural tempo, using his back to store and give back energy. This is wonderful information, but it presents a problem. For the most part, there is no direct way to influence stride, tempo, or energy on a green horse without the risk of adversely affecting them also. But we can use *direction* to create *angle,* which encourages *bend,* and then use angle and bend to regulate stride, tempo, and energy.

You can use direction to compel a horse to move at an angle to the line of travel he's on by putting him on a circle so small he cannot bend enough to match the circumference. The most common example of turning a horse on this small a circle is when you turn a horse around in a barn aisle. He will either swing his quarters around his forehand, his forehand around his quarters, or both around each other. He has to. Horses cannot bend enough to walk on the circumference of a circle small enough to fit in a typical barn aisle.

Advantages of Lateral Movement

Having a horse move laterally helps to regulate speed, engages the horse's hind legs, and encourages him to bend.

We need lateral movement to regulate speed in early training, because a horse on his forehand is a little like a wheel rolling down a hill.

We need lateral movement to regulate speed in early training, because a horse on his forehand is a little like a wheel rolling down a hill. It's going to continue to go faster and faster until it becomes unstable. Since horses can't go very fast when they move at an angle to the line they are on, you can balance the forward movement with lateral movement to get to optimum speed.

A horse moving laterally has to bring his inside hind leg under himself while lifting his weight and the rider's. This strengthens his hind legs, which, over time, allows him to accept more weight on them. It is only by acceptance of more weight on his hind legs that a horse can lift himself off his forehand.

Advantages of Bend

If you keep your horse on circle so small he has to move at an angle to his line of travel for a little while, he will discover the easiest way to move at an angle is to bend his body. In fact, the more he bends, the easier it becomes. You don't even need a horse to test this. Stand with your back as straight and stiff as possible and take a lateral step by crossing your right leg in front of your left leg. You'll find the movement is awkward and difficult. If you now bend your body with the movement by stretching the left side of your body up so that your left shoulder is higher than your right while taking another lateral step, you'll find the movement has become easy and graceful. Horses demonstrate the same awkwardness when their backs are stiff and the same grace when they are relaxed and bending.

In the above example you "bent your body" to the right by stretching your left side, but there is another way of accomplishing bend in your body or your horse's—one to be avoided. It is possible to bend to the right by compressing or shortening to the right. If you try to take a lateral step while pulling your right shoulder down, instead of stretching your left shoulder up, the movement is not fluid and easy and the advantage of bending is lost. So when we bend the horse (or you, in some of the other unmounted exercises coming up!) we always bend by stretching the outside of the body. Creating bend by stretching the outside rather than by collapsing the inside is always correct for the horse and always correct for you.

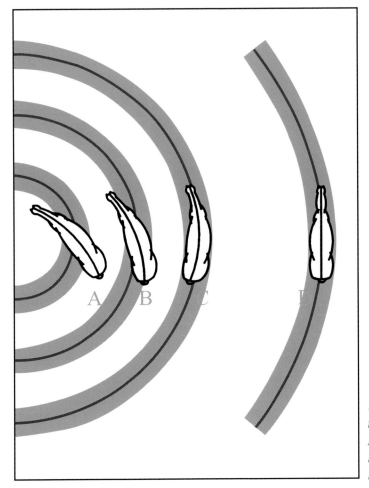

Figure 25 As the size of the circle increases (A to D), the need for the horse to bend and move laterally decreases.

The "Natural" Circle

As I said earlier, directing a horse on to a circle so small he has to move at an angle to the line he's on has the advantages of reducing his speed, engaging his hind leg, and encouraging him to relax and bend his back. But if the circle is too small, he can't swing his legs freely in their natural tempo. If the circle is too big, there is no incentive for him to move at an angle, or bend his body.

Figure 25 illustrates this. Horse A is on a circle so small he has to go around it at a big angle to the line. It shows him it's easier to move laterally if

101

For every horse at every gait there is a circle of a certain diameter on which all the elements of movement come into true balance. I call it a Natural Circle.

he bends his back, but it doesn't allow free movement in his natural tempo. At the other extreme, horse D is on a circle so large he can go around and around on it for years and years (as so many horses have) without ever learning to bend and soften in his body. Horse C would, at first glance, seem to be right on target. He's on a circle that he can bend to stay on. Indeed, with a horse that already understands how to bend and will offer it, this is the ideal. However, with horses not yet accustomed to bending, it is not as helpful as the circle horse B is on.

Horse B is on a circle just a little smaller than horse C. To stay on this circle, horse B has to move with a slight angle to the line, which encourages him to engage and bend. In fact, just working on this circle helps him to find the correct balance of bend, speed, forward, and lateral movement while encouraging him to move in his natural tempo and swing his legs.

For every horse at every gait there is a circle of a certain diameter on which all the elements of movement come into true balance. I call it a *Natural Circle.*

15

Your Natural Circle

The Natural Circle helps your horse to find his true balance, and the best way to help your horse find his Natural Circle is to know how you feel moving on your own Natural Circle.

Yes, people have Natural Circles too. In fact, nature has left you a clue to help find your Natural Circle. The clue you have is that when you are moving freely on your Natural Circle, your inside leg will tend to swing out so that your inside foot lands in front of your outside foot (fig. 26). If the circle is too small your leg will not swing freely. If it is too large, your inside leg won't swing out enough to be noticeable.

To use this clue and find your Natural Circle, mark the center of a circle. Now walk five or six feet away from the mark. Turn left or right and walk casually on the circle with the radius you've just paced out. This does not have to be precise. If your inside leg swings directly in front of your outside leg, this is a Natural Circle for you. If it doesn't, try walking on a larger or smaller circle until it does.

Once you have established your Natural Circle, you can use it to get some feeling of riding a horse on his Natural Circle. Walking normally on your circle, bend your body by stretching up on the side that is on the inside of the circle.

Figure 26 When walking on your "Natural Circle," your inside leg will swing in front of your outside leg.

If you continue to let your legs swing freely (just "follow your feet!") your outside foot will begin to land in front of the inside, and the circle gets smaller. You are "falling in." The feeling of falling in on your circle is similar in many ways to the feeling of sitting on a horse that is falling in. Also note the very slight change required to go from being balanced to falling in is very much like the slight change that will cause a horse to fall in.

It's possible to experience "falling out" from your circle as well. Walk on your Natural Circle again with your body straight. Now bend by stretching up on the outside. This slight bend in your body caused by stretching up will cause your inside leg to swing further out, and the circle will expand. You are falling out. This is very much the sensation a rider gets when the horse falls out over his shoulder.

To feel what it's like to balance a horse's bend, lateral and forward motion, you need to balance your bend, forward, and lateral motion. To do this, go back on to the circumference of your Natural Circle. Start by walking naturally again and then turn your body inward slightly (point your belly button a little in toward the center of the circle) so that you're moving at an angle to the line of the circumference—your line of travel. As you change your angle to the line of travel, bend your body by stretching up just a little as you did to fall out in the above exercise. If you have the correct angle to your line and the right amount of bend, you will stay on the same size circle. Your bend, forward, and lateral motion are in balance.

Once your bend, forward, and lateral motion are in balance, you can find other feelings to explore. The first is that it will seem effortless to continue on the circle you're on. If you try to make the circle larger or smaller, it will take an additional effort on your part, as though there is some strange, mystical force holding you on your circle. In fact, there are forces keeping you on the circle, but they're not strange or mystical. They're just the laws of physics and biomechanics at work.

Notice that you are displacing your hip and bending your body in the same way that made you fall out in the previous exercise, but with the added lateral component, you stay on the circle. It has become a controlled falling out, in a manner of speaking. This is very similar to the feeling of a young horse moving from the rider's inside leg to, but not through, the outside rein. (This feeling is subtler in advanced horses.)

Another observation you can make is that it's easy to move on your circle this way when you let your legs swing; however, you must make an effort to take shorter steps. Also, if you try to take slower or faster steps, the movement that was easy and fluid becomes forced, stiff, and awkward. This is the Natural Circle encouraging you to move at your natural tempo with a free, swinging stride. However, if you allow your legs to swing out in longer strides, you will find that the movement remains easy, your bend and angle remain essentially the same, but the circle you're walking on will expand. You have gone from your Natural Circle for your normal or working gait to your Natural Circle for your extended gait.

Light, almost delicate aids are what good riding is all about!

Before moving on from these ground exercises, I would like to add one personal note for each of you. I know you have read the preceding paragraphs and probably think they're interesting, but you may not do the exercises because you'll feel silly walking around on a little circle trying to feel these things. Well, I can tell you for a fact that in the absence of a fully trained schoolmaster and instructor capable of standing there and guiding you through each ride, this is absolutely the best way to get the idea of what "correct" feels like. If, for a moment, you imagine your hips as the horse's shoulders, you can almost "feel" or visualize the very slight displacement of weight that causes the horse to fall in or out. It becomes easy to judge how light the aids for guiding your horse along any path can be. This is the ideal. Light, almost delicate aids are what good riding is about! Doing these exercises will literally save years of floundering about on your horse trying to stumble upon the right feeling. Now, don't you feel silly for not having done them already?

Of course, some will say that people bend vertically, and horses horizontally, therefore the so-called Natural Circle does not apply in training horses. It is true that horses have very different biomechanics than people, but there are a surprising number of similarities as well. It is also true that the laws of physics are exactly the same for people and horses. In fact, I first realized that Natural Circles existed when I was on horseback, where the feelings and effects are more obvious. It was only when I tried to find ways of explaining and demonstrating it to others that I discovered the same could be felt on the ground, with no horse at all.

———————

16 Your Horse's Natural Circle

Now that you have the real feeling of walking on your own Natural Circle, it's possible to imagine how this will come together when you ride him on his Natural Circle after you have done the preparatory ground exercises with him.

The first time you sit on your horse while he walks on his Natural Circle, you will immediately notice that the circle is very small—perhaps only five or six meters in diameter. Early on, his steps will be tentative, the bend and the angle to the line of travel will be inconsistent, and you will probably have to stop and begin again several times. After a few minutes, though, the horse will start to feel how comfortable it is to work on the circle, and as the forces you felt on the circle begin to affect him, he will settle. Usually, you can feel the horse relax; often he will snort a bit as he does. Then, he will start to take longer, looser strides and the circle will seem to expand on its own, just as your circle expanded when you took longer strides.

At that point, you will be able to ask for the trot (some horses will offer the trot on their own). Again, the steps will be tentative at first, but after a little while, the horse will adjust his angle and bend to find his balance. He will start to relax and take longer strides. As in the walk, the circle will expand as the strides lengthen; however, it will still be a small circle—maybe only eight to twelve meters. Of course I'm only guessing when I say eight to twelve meters. As the definition of a Natural Circle says, it will be different for each horse at each gait. You will have to feel the circle and help guide him to it.

These ideas differ dramatically from ideas proposed in other books on training. To allow the horse to find the circle, angle, and bend that are easiest for him to balance himself on, opposes the conventional wisdom to work on a particular, and to my thinking arbitrary, size of circle—with an even bend and no angle to the line. You should certainly be able to do that eventually, but for now your goal is to show your horse how to balance his movement. Why not teach him about true balance on the circle and with the angle and bend which is the most "natural" for him to find it?

...being ridden is difficult; therefore, a horse needs to be shown the easiest way to carry a rider so that his task becomes easier.

Another idea that is not conventional is that he will find the easiest circle to work on to be rather small. My goodness! This isn't just unconventional—it's heresy! After all, everybody "knows" that it's easier for a horse to be on a large circle than a small one, just as everybody "knows" that working on small circles is advanced and hard on the hocks, while working on great big circles is elementary and "easy."

Well, being ridden is never "easy" at all. A central theme of this book is that being ridden is difficult; therefore, a horse needs to be shown the easiest way to carry a rider so that his task becomes easier.

Now, which is easier for the horse? Spending a little time on a small circle that shows him how to balance a rider and use himself correctly, or spending years on a large circle and never learning either? Is it easier on the horse to be guided gently into bending and balancing by the same forces of physics and biomechanics you felt on your Natural Circle, or to have a rider sitting on his back trying to bend him by pulling in his mouth and trying to send him forward by kicking him in his ribs? Is it easier on the hocks to develop the muscles that support them so the stress is relieved, or to let the full weight of horse and rider grind the delicate cartilage until there is nothing left but bone scraping bone?

These questions must be answered in the context of Rule Number 2—*Reward in Proportion* (p. 21). Being ridden is difficult. For a horse that isn't already strengthened and made supple by correct work, being ridden is extremely difficult. Such a horse can only be worked for a few minutes at a time before being allowed a rest. Some can only work for moments at a time. However, with time, the muscles do strengthen and the horse does learn to balance the rider correctly. As the horse's strength, balance, and coordination increase, so does the amount of time that he can be worked.

Increases in strength, balance, and coordination are the benefits of riding small circles for short periods in early training. Work in true balance that includes bend and lateral movement, keeps the horse's back relaxed so he can use it correctly to store and return energy, which in turn, strengthens it. Consistently allowing him to move at the angle to the line he needs to be on to keep in true balance, encourages the horse to bring his inside hind under, and lift his body, Lifting the body strengthens the muscles correctly so they can support the weight of horse and rider (and also protects the hock joints). The work in natural tempo teaches the horse to swing his legs freely, so he begins to understand what balancing the weight of a rider while moving freely forward feels like. As he develops strength, understanding, and feel, he also develops the coordination required to maintain balance consistently. So, as the horse develops understanding and ability, he can maintain the same balance developed on his Natural Circle on progressively larger circles.

Which is easier for the horse? Spending a little time on a small circle that shows him how to balance a rider and use himself correctly, or spending years on a large circle and never learning either?

The method for going from small to progressively larger circles is to balance your horse on his Natural Circle first and then let the circle expand. In actual practice, there will be many times when the circle gets too large for the horse to maintain his balance, and you will have to lead him back to a smaller circle to restore it.

And here is yet another very important point. By returning to a smaller circle to rebalance the horse, you are able to use aids that release by simply riding him forward onto the smaller circle. I'll describe the exact aids used in Chapter 19, *Under Saddle and On To the Aids*; the point to remember now is that by using the balancing effects of the correct size circle, you never have to pull back on your horse's mouth to adjust bend, balance, tempo, or stride.

By allowing the circle to expand when the horse is balanced and by riding forward onto a smaller circle to restore balance, you can eventually ride him on a circle so large it is essentially a straight line. To visualize this, imagine being balanced on the small circle in the center of figure 27, going to the right. Over time, your horse will be able to maintain his balance working fur-

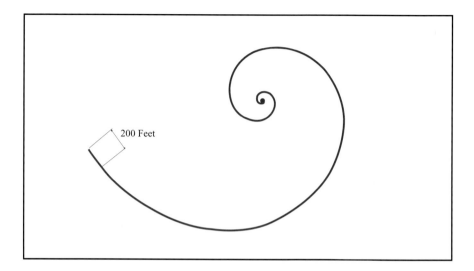

Figure 27 *By allowing the circle to expand when the horse is balanced, you can eventually ride him in the same balance on a circle so large that it is essentially a straight line.*

ther and further out on the curve until he is at the very left edge. Looking at the diagram, it's easy to view riding that portion of the curve as just a large circle; however, the scale is deceiving. The last section of the curve on the left edge (marked on the diagram) represents 200 feet of distance (about the length of a dressage ring centerline) and the amount of curve is less then a width of a hoof. Still, the horse is ridden with a degree of bend to help maintain balance much the same way he used his bend to help stay balanced on the small circle in the center.

To maintain balance with a young horse on this large a curve or straight line, it may be necessary to have a significant angle to the line as well as a considerable bend in his body. That's fine. It doesn't make any difference if your horse needs more angle and bend to balance his motion because as long as he is in true balance, he's working in his natural tempo, his stride is free-swinging, and his back is being strengthened.

As the horse gains strength, he'll be able to lift his back (bend it up) and accept more weight on his hind legs. As he takes more weight on his rear legs, his weight becomes evenly distributed. As his weight becomes evenly distributed, he won't need as much bend, and the bend he does have will become even from poll to dock. When his weight is equal and his bend is even, he won't need to travel at an angle to his line to maintain true balance. He can go in working gaits. By continuing to ride him in the working gaits, he'll become stronger and more balanced, and soon, he'll be capable of accepting more weight on his hind legs than his front. Then you're ready to begin half-halts and collection.

Of course the goal is, and always has been, to make the horse capable of carrying a rider in balance. But balance is not just a singular question of weight on front and rear legs. It cannot be—if it was, you could never balance a horse. You cannot lift a horse off his forehand with your hands because you will only succeed in discouraging him from using his back, which in turn prevents him from using his hind legs to accept weight. You cannot push a horse up to the bit with your legs because if your horse doesn't already know how to carry you and hasn't already been made so strong and supple that he freely offers to lift you correctly, your legs are just poking him in the ribs, tightening his body, and again, discouraging him from using his back correctly. However, when you think of balance as the true balance of motion, and temporarily sacrifice circles of arbitrary size, even bend, and keeping your horse on his line—then the balance of weight on all four feet and a free-swinging stride are given to you.

You cannot lift a horse off his forehand with your hands because you will only succeed in discouraging him from using his back.

Indeed, it is because of true balance that we virtually always ride a horse bent evenly from poll to dock, even when on straight lines. The conventional wisdom that we always ride them bent because their shoulders are narrower than their hips, is nothing more than a happy coincidence. Horses are ridden evenly bent as though always on a circle, because the slight bend is still used in the balance of motion, even after balance of weight is attained.

PART FOUR

Little by Little

~ ~

17

First Touch

Whether you're starting a baby or working with an older horse that has already has been ridden for years, he has to be relaxed in his body and mind. This part provides exercises you can use to tell him about everything explained in the first few chapters of this book. Show him that you're playing with him on his terms and the hour or so a day you spend with him is the most interesting and pleasant part of his day. Explain to him the exercise-reward cycle and let him know that he will be rewarded for his efforts. Of course, it's very important that you make it clear nobody gets hurt, and if he does make a mistake, you will correct him but not punish him. Just take your time and make sure he understands these concepts.

Herding

To introduce him to these concepts, you are going to use some simple ground exercises. We call these exercises *leading* and *ground tying,* but your horse will think he is being *herded.* These are great exercises to teach the early concepts because every horse already knows how to be herded. Being herded is one of the first things mothers teach foals. They learn from their mothers to be aware of body language and to go, stop, turn, or stand when "told" to. Because every horse has already been taught to be herded, these simple ground exercises are the great equalizers. Whether a horse is a totally green baby, a good old trooper who does his best, or a rather rebellious sort, you can use these exercises to establish your role as leader of the herd. As you do, you will gain your horse's attention and trust.

As leading is a simple matter that anyone can teach any horse in little time, the horse begins the process of learning to learn. In many cases these simple ground exercises are a horse's first exposure to the exercise-reward cycle. If you recall from Chapter 2, we used the example of teaching a dog to sit to explain the exercise-reward cycle and the basic training process. First we ask correctly, then we make correct, and then we reward. Use these exercises to teach the horse that he is being spoken to, that you are trying to communicate, and that the exercise-reward cycle is the method of communication you use.

He has elected you boss, put you in charge, made you leader and parent. He has given you his trust, and now it is yours to cultivate or lose.

Latching On

These exercises are a method of establishing you as the dominant member of the herd without much fuss. By simply having the horse walk when you walk and stop when you stop, he learns to submit to your leadership. It teaches him to pay attention and to watch for subtle changes in your actions and body language.

This produces some very interesting behavior in these early lessons. Somewhere during the first session, the horse will begin to sniff at you, nuzzle you, and perhaps even try to smell your breath (fig. 28). All of his attention will be directed on you from that point on. Bombs could go off just outside the ring, and rather than jump, run, and find his own way to safety, he may jump, but then he is going to stop and look to you for guidance. He has elected you boss, put you in charge, made you leader and parent. He has given you his trust, and now it is yours to cultivate or lose.

Once this happens, (and it should within the first hour), the horse is going to *latch on*. I can't explain this other than to say that it "feels" as though there is a magnetic force of sorts between the horse and me when I'm close to him and, if I move away, I can feel the force break. The longer I work the ground exercises with him, the stronger the feeling and the farther away I have to go before it breaks. I have no explanation for the metaphysician or parapsy-

Figure 28 Somewhere during the first session, the horse will begin to sniff at you, nuzzle you, and perhaps even try to smell your breath. This shows he is attaching himself to you and electing you leader.

chologist, and I offer no apology to the rationalist. It's simply a feeling I get, and if I'm to believe the description of my students, they have horses latch on to them too. I assume that anyone else who takes the time to work with a horse in this manner will experience it as well.

All of the above-described benefits are reasons for spending time working with a horse on these elementary ground exercises. The following descriptions of each are offered in a fairly arbitrary order. It will be the handler's decision to teach a horse that is fidgety to stand quietly first, or to teach a lethargic subject to lead first. Each exercise is described with the handler on the left (near) side of the horse, but it is important that they are taught from the right (off) side as well.

Tack

The particular tack used for these exercises isn't that important. When beginning it's best to use a longe line made from wide soft cotton web as a lead. Attach it to either the bridle or halter so that if the horse tries to escape, you can let him go away from you without losing complete control. I'll work a young unbroken horse in only a halter and longe line. (With a foal about ten days old I'll put his mother on the cross-ties and do these exercises with baby in the barn aisle. Five minutes a day for a few days in a row and your baby will be well mannered for life!) For a horse that's already been ridden and is being re-schooled, you can use a bridle with a fat snaffle. If using a bridle, run the longe line through the inside snaffle ring, over the poll, and attach to the outside ring. This way, the pressure is only put on the corners of the mouth, not the bars. Once your horse latches on you can replace the longe line with a lead on the halter or just use the reins if bridled. Eventually, your horse should become so good at this that you won't need anything and will be able to take off the lead or leave the reins draped over his neck. Why not? His mother didn't use tack!

It is best to have a dressage whip about 40-inches long while doing these exercises. In all of the leading exercises described in this chapter, the whip should be held in the hand away from the horse (your left hand when on the horse's left side).

Blowing Off Steam

If the horse just stands around when work begins: Great! He'll be moving soon enough, and moving correctly as well. On the other hand, if the horse is really high and full of himself, then it's fine to allow him to let off excess energy at the beginning of the early lessons.

The trick to having a horse let off energy is to be sure that he does let it off and not build it up. Some horses will start to work themselves up into more of a frenzy if allowed to run around on the end of a longe line. If this happens, your horse needs to be stopped. When stopping a horse running at the end of a longe line, rather than try to pull him to a halt, use the wall of

Figure 29 **To stop a horse running at the end of the longe line, lead him to the wall of the arena or fence line.**

the arena or a fence line to do the job. As the horse is coming around the circle, warn him with a give-and-take on the longe line that he is about to be stopped and then lead him into the wall or the fence (fig. 29).

Once the horse has stopped, keep him standing still. He has had his chance to blow up, and now it is school time. You determine when he moves and when he stands. However, if at any point during this early stage the horse gets aggressive and tries to bite, kick, or charge you, do not be aggressive back. You may give him a light tap on the nose with your hand, touch him with the whip on his flank (just to show him you could have hit him if you wanted to), or you can simply get out of his way and let him run a bit more if necessary. After he realizes you're not going to try to hurt or fight with him, you can stop him and begin again.

Of course, I don't expect your horse to become aggressive here if he hasn't been aggressive before. Quite to the contrary. I've used the philosophy and training methods described in this book to take many recalcitrant horses and turn them into pleasant partners, quite happy in their work. However, it doesn't happen immediately, and during the re-schooling period you have to be aware of the possibilities and be prepared to take the correct course of action.

There are also some horses that may get nervous or tense as this work proceeds. You can allow them an occasional period at the end of the longe line to calm down too. Also note that just as there is a difference between a correction and an aid, there is a big difference between letting a tense horse get the edge off by running around at the end of a longe line and correct longeing. As you will see in Chapter 18, for a horse to be longeing correctly he has to be soft, bending, and relaxed.

Leading

My method of leading is to have the horse's shoulder parallel to mine so that his head and neck are in front of me (fig. 30). There are a few reasons why I want the horse in this position. First, it is the safest position to be in—out of range of the horse's rear legs and far enough from the head that if he swings it around, you can get out of the way before it hits you. If a horse rears while you are working him from the ground, you simply need to stay at his shoulder and you won't end up under his front feet.

Another reason that I lead from this position is that I do all the *in-hand* exercises (see Chapter 18) from this position too. I also like working a horse from the ground with his head and neck in front of me because that is where they are when I ride him. He has to be looking forward and paying attention to me while I'm sitting behind his withers when riding, so I get him used to the idea now.

This is not the only acceptable method of having a horse lead. For instance, the Pony Club suggests holding the reins in both hands and keeping the horse's nose parallel to your shoulder. Many Western trainers suggest that the horse should be directly behind you while being led. For their purposes, their methods make sense, and I'm not suggesting that they change. I am saying that regardless of which method you have been using, for the purpose of getting the most benefit of the methods in this book, teach your horse to lead as I am describing.

Figure 30 **Teach your horse to stay at your shoulder while you are leading him.**

To get the horse to lead, stand at his shoulder with the lead in your right hand and the whip in your left hand, click softly, and begin to walk. If the horse does not walk with you, give him a light tap on his flank with the whip. Once he begins to move, pat him near the withers and tell him "Good Boy." After a few strides, stop walking. If the horse stops with you, pat and praise him again. If not, softly say the word "Whoa," and give some gentle tugs on the lead. These tugs should be more like taps than pulls. They are a signal to ask the horse to stop, not a mechanical means of pulling the horse to a halt.

If the horse does not understand, continue the gentle tugs and walk straight into a wall or fence so he has to stop. The goal of this exercise is to get the horse to watch you and follow your body language, not to make him submit to being pulled to a halt. So first you ask him to halt by halting yourself, and then, if necessary give him a few gentle tugs or walk him into a wall to make him stop correctly.

The ideal is to always have the horse stop so that his shoulder is next to your shoulder and you are both looking ahead in the same direction. Usually when the horse is first taught this lesson, he won't just stop when you do, he will try to position himself so he is facing you. Rather than waste effort repositioning the horse, reposition yourself so that no matter what the horse does, his shoulder is always at yours. Horses are very reasonable fellows, and they shortly figure out that there is no point in standing anywhere other than at your shoulder. Whenever he does, give him a pat and a rest.

Turning the Horse Toward You

After the horse has figured out that he should stay at your shoulder, it is time to begin work on turning. To have the horse turn toward you, begin by walking on a circle with the horse on the outside. Gradually decrease the size of the circle (fig. 31). As the circle gets smaller, the horse has to swing his body around to keep his shoulders next to yours. As he does, and he will if the leading lesson was taught correctly, he will tend to swing his quarters around his forehand—his quarters will be on a larger circle then his forehand. Of course we're not looking for a precise movement (after all you've only been working with him for ten minutes now), just so long as he swings his hindquarters out as he turns into you.

Turn Away From You

To give the horse the idea of turning away from you, simply start walking the horse forward and then move in a circle to your right with your right hand up and sort of "shooing" him away from you (fig. 32). It may be necessary to give him an occasional "tweak" on the nose (just a light tap with your fingers), until he gets the idea of turning away.

Start off on a fairly big circle to the right—15 meters wide or so. Very soon, usually within several minutes, the horse will begin to get the idea that he should continue to keep his shoulder near yours even though you're moving into him, so he will move his shoulders away from you and in on the circle. When he does, you can gradually decrease the size of the circle (fig. 33).

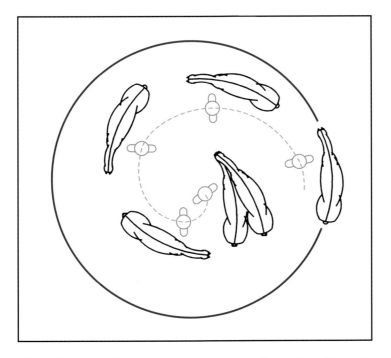

Figure 31 *As you lead your horse on to a smaller and smaller circle he will try to stay next to you. This results in him doing a rudimentary turn-on-the-forehand.*

As the circumference becomes too small for the horse to walk normally on it, he has to move laterally. Since he is already moving his shoulders away from you, he will begin to swing his shoulders around his hindquarters.

Ground Tying

When the horse begins to understand that he should go when you go and stop when you stop, you can also teach him to stand while you move away. Technically, this can only be called *ground tying*. Yes, this is typically used by Western riders, but I wonder why they should have the sole rights to it because it is so useful!

Figure 32 **To walk on a circle with your horse on the inside of you, "shoo" him away from you with the inside hand.**

It is incredibly convenient to have a horse stand quietly for a few moments while you go to pick up the fly spray, whip, gloves, or any of the other many little necessities that go along with horses. It is simple to teach, and aside from being useful in the practical sense, it has another benefit that should not be overlooked: it expands the rider's sphere of influence. There is a significant psychological change in a horse that submits to a rider's wish although the rider is several feet away or even out of sight altogether.

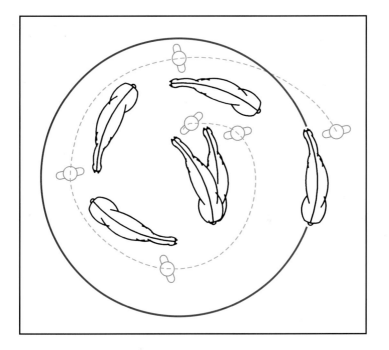

Figure 33 Turn your horse away from you as you walk on to a smaller and smaller circle. When the circle gets small enough he will have to swing his forehand around his quarters in a rudimentary turn-on-the-haunches.

I had a particularly willful horse in for training, and due to his nature I probably did a lot more of this early ground schooling than even I consider normal. When he was at the point where I could leave him in front of the barn, go up to the house, get a drink, and come back to find him in the exact same spot, it was time to move on and begin the rest of his schooling.

Start to teach the horse to ground tie while the longe line is still attached to the halter or bridle. From the stop, pat him on the nose lightly and let enough line out so that it falls to the ground just in front of him. Tell him to "Stand", and step backward away from him (fig. 34). (The pat on the nose and use of the word "stand" are to let the horse know he should not follow along

Figure 34 *Start to teach your horse to ground-tie with the longe line still attached. Tell him to "stand," give him a pat on the nose, and then back away from him.*

as though being led.) If he stands quietly for a second or two, go back up and reward. Over a period of just a few days, this lesson—incorporated with the others—should allow you to step back the full length of the longe line while the horse just stands there, quietly waiting for the next instruction. As time goes on, the longe can be replaced with a lead that is released altogether. The final step is to have him stand with the lead draped over his neck, very much like the reins dropped on his neck, and similar to the way you will drop them on his neck for the *allowed stop*. (I first discussed the allowed stop in Chapter 4 and will explain it in detail in Chapter 22.)

Desensitization to Extraneous External Stimuli

I know Western trainers refer to this process as "*sacking out*," but since I'm supposed to be a fancy dressage rider I gave this part what I think is a rather more catchy title.

As I said before, one element of getting your horse's trust is to let him know he is not going to be hurt. To teach him that, touch him without hurting him. It doesn't have to be anything special, just touch him a lot. Before a horse can be trained, he has to be touched, and there is just no way around this. He cannot fear you. He must accept and trust you. This may seem an elementary matter; however there are a large percentage of horses that don't really accept their trainer.

A horse that does not accept his trainer is afraid of his trainer. Often, people think they are doing a frightened horse a favor by trying not to scare him more and staying as unobtrusive as possible. This is reversed logic. The horse is already scared to death! The longer he goes without being touched, the more afraid he becomes that he will be touched. The best thing to do for this type of horse is to get past his fear and show him that he is not going to be hurt. The only way to do this is to touch him without hurting him. Get the horse over his initial fear and he will discover that he likes it. There isn't a horse in the world that doesn't have a spot that he actually adores having rubbed. Use that. Find his favorite spot, his next favorite, and the one after that.

Once the horse has been touched all over his body with your hands, show him that the whip is just an extension of the hand. Go through the process again, and touch him all over with the whip. Show him he still doesn't get hurt. This is especially important with horses being re-schooled, because they are virtually all afraid of the whip. Unfortunately, they usually have reason to be afraid as well. After that, the process can be repeated with a towel, a longe line, or a feather duster for that matter. It doesn't make any difference; he is just being shown that anything we touch him with is safe. He is learning he is safe with us. This process is the start of the relationship.

All of the above exercises can be taught in approximately one hour. Yes, that's right. Within sixty minutes you can teach a horse to go, stop, stand, and turn toward or away from you with nothing more than a halter, lead, and

A horse that does not accept his trainer is afraid of his trainer.

There isn't a horse in the world that doesn't have a spot that he actually adores having rubbed. Use that.

these few techniques. None of the results will be perfect at first, but by repeating the lessons for a few days, they'll improve dramatically.

The importance of these early lessons cannot be stressed enough. The horse has learned to trust you and to watch you for instruction and guidance. He has learned to go, stop, stand, and turn. He has learned the exercise-reward cycle—that you are the giver of reward, and being around you is fun. He has learned that playing with you is an interesting part of his day.

18 Soften, Bend, and Move Into the Hand

Once your horse is leading and standing quietly, it is time to teach him to soften in the jaw, poll, neck, and body and then to balance himself on a curve and move from the inside leg to the outside hand. The best way to accomplish these goals is through *work in hand*. Work in hand can be defined as any exercise where the trainer is on the ground, holding the reins and asking the horse to react to the aids as though being ridden. In a sense it is "riding" the horse from the ground, the difference being that your leg is simulated by the dressage whip, and you cannot use your seat as an aid.

Work in hand allows you to build on the leading exercises from last chapter. It's a natural progression for the horse to go from simply following you and moving where you say, to moving precisely the way you say. Work in hand also allows you to keep an objective point of view since you're observing the horse and his reactions from the ground. Another advantage is that this work allows you an opportunity to learn what a horse reacting correctly to the aids feels like, while at the same time it allows the horse to learn how to react to the aids correctly without having to deal with the weight of a rider. It gives him a chance to feel how to move correctly without having to cope with balancing extra weight. This is important because the horse will already be busy learning at least two major concepts in each exercise.

At this stage, it's impossible to only teach one thing at a time because everything we are teaching is so interrelated. For instance, teaching the horse to soften in the jaw, poll, and neck is also teaching him how to accept contact. The two cannot be separated because we have no method of teaching one without the other. By substituting a light touch of our hand or whip where our inside leg will be when we ride, we're able to teach the horse to soften in his body at the same time we teach him to move from the leg. We need to do it this way because teaching him to move from the leg is the only means available to teach him to relax in his body. The horse will learn to balance himself at the same time he's learning to bend and move from the inside leg to the outside hand because that is the only way we have of helping the horse find his correct balance on a circle, and correct work on the circle is the only way we have to teach him to move softly into the hand. In addition, during this time the horse is still confirming his understanding of the exercise–reward cycle and learning to trust you—so don't underestimate the complexity and importance of the training going on in these exercises. There is a tremendous amount of information being transmitted during this phase.

Tack

To work your horse in hand, he should be in a bridle with a fat snaffle. You will need a dressage whip about 40-inches long. If you're comfortable that your horse has "latched on" and is going to stay attentive to you, then a longe line is optional. If you don't want to risk losing control over him, run it through the inside bit ring, over his poll, and attach it to the outside bit ring.

The noseband (a plain cavesson) on the bridle should be fairly loose. By fairly loose, I mean that you should be able to slip two fingers under it easily. If any noseband is tight, it forces the horse's mouth shut and he never learns to relax his jaw and allow his mouth to close quietly on the bit.

In fact, when re-schooling a horse that has been ridden with a very tight noseband, it's often advisable to remove the noseband altogether while the horse is learning how to soften in his jaw, poll, and neck correctly. Yes, a horse with this background will probably spend some time opening his mouth and sticking his tongue out. However, the open mouth and tongue sticking out are only symptoms of the real problem—he never learned to accept contact correctly. As you proceed through the re-schooling process, he'll realize that opening his mouth or sticking out his tongue doesn't make him more comfortable, but if he relaxes, you will allow him to stretch out to the bit and take the amount of contact he is comfortable with. Then the symptoms of an open mouth and tongue sticking out will slowly go away.

General Instructions for Work in Hand

During these exercises you will always be bending the horse toward you, so you are always going to be on the inside of the horse's bend, and the rein on your side will be the *inside* rein. The rein on the other side is the *outside* rein.

In the previous chapter, *First Touch* it was the trainer's choice to select the order in which the exercises were taught. However, the early work-in-hand exercises should be done in the order presented and on both sides of the horse before going on to the next exercise. The horse must clearly understand each exercise and perform it willingly and easily before proceeding to the next one because each successive exercise depends on the one before it.

The order of the exercises is set because the horse has to learn to soften in the jaw, poll, and neck in response to the reins, and then to soften in his body and move away from the whip before he can accept contact and move freely. So we start by softening him at the front (jaw) and work toward the back (his body), and then we can ask him to move freely forward on his Natural Circle.

You need to soften the horse from front to back before asking him to move, because only when a horse's back is relaxed and he is using it correctly can you ride him (or "work" him in the case of in-hand exercises) from "back to front." Riding a horse from back to front means that the energy of the horse's hind legs is coming through his body and he is being guided gently by your aids. Although advanced horses and a very, very small percentage of green horses may relax their backs if the rider simply asks for more energy, the overwhelming majority of horses will get more tense, stiffen their backs, and take faster, shorter, choppier strides if you ask for more energy before they are relaxed. So although I absolutely want you riding your horse from back to front, it is only after he has been softened from "front to back" that he can relax and let the energy come through his body. Once this happens, he can move with looseness, freedom, and balance.

...only when a horse's back is relaxed and he is using it correctly can you ride him or "work" him from "back to front."

Exercises to Soften the Jaw, Poll, and Neck

So, to start at the front, the first in-hand exercises (often called *flexions*) teach the horse to accept contact correctly, and they are used to relax the horse's muscles in his jaw, poll, and neck.

All a horse needs to learn about contact with the bit is that he should soften in his jaw, poll, and neck when the rider, or handler working the horse in hand, picks up the reins and draws back on them just enough so that he can feel the bit. He is "touching" the bit through the reins. That is all contact is, just touching. It's not pulling, leaning, squeezing, supporting, or bracing. Just touching. The horse should seek contact with the rider through the bit and rein. When he finds it, he should soften so that he and the rider are just touching each other.

Begin this first in-hand exercise by standing at the horse's shoulder. Working from the left side as shown in figure 35, take the outside (right) rein in your right hand, and bring it around the neck so you are holding it near the withers. When the outside rein is held this way, you can just hold the rein and relax your arm so that the weight of your arm creates the contact. It's also possible to increase the contact on the outside of the bit by bringing your hand down, or to soften the contact by bringing your hand up.

The *inside* (left) rein is brought over the back of your *inside* hand and under your thumb. Adjust the rein so you have contact when you rest your hand on the horse (fig. 36). I generally prefer to put my left hand up by the horse's poll as shown in figure 36, but it's absolutely acceptable to put your hand on his cheekbone as shown in figure 37. To increase the contact, pivot your hand so your little finger comes away from the horse, or soften the contact by letting it rest flat on him again. The rein used in this fashion directs the pressure of the bit up to the corner of his mouth toward his poll.

Once you have the reins held correctly, pivot your inside hand a little to create a pressure that is mildly unpleasant for the horse. Usually the horse will attempt to get rid of the unpleasant sensation by tossing his head up, pulling on the reins, twisting his head left or right, and sometimes by backing up. Since you're steadying your hand on his cheek or poll, you'll be able to maintain a steady pressure during all of this (fig. 38). If instead of avoiding the pressure by moving his head, your horse takes a strong hold of the bit and stiffens, vary the contact on the inside rein a little until he begins to relax.

Allowed Stop From the Ground
Regardless of how the horse reacts at first, eventually he'll relax a little and drop his head. At the very moment he does, release both reins, drop them on his neck, pat him, step back, and let him rest for a few moments (fig. 39).

This release, pat, and rest are a form of the *allowed stop,* which was discussed in Chapter 4. By teaching your horse now, while working from the ground, that he is allowed to stop when you drop the reins and pat him, he will associate the same actions with reward when you do them from the saddle later.

Softening the Horse's Jaw and Poll (Figures 35, 36, 37, and 38)

*Figure 35 **Bring the right rein over the neck, hold it in your hand and let the weight of your arm set the contact.***

Figure 36 **Bring the inside rein up toward the horse's ear. This puts tension on the bit on the inside corner of his mouth, while the outside rein prevents him from over bending his neck.**

Figure 37 If you find it difficult to reach your horse's poll, bring the inside rein over the back of your hand and brace on his cheekbone. This method also puts pressure on the corner of his mouth.

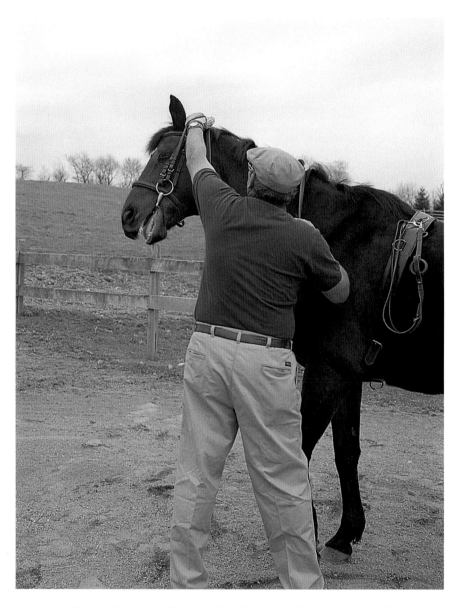

Figure 38 *By steadying your hand on his cheek or poll, like this, you'll be able to maintain a steady pressure if your horse attempts to get rid of the rein pressure by tossing or twisting his head, and pulling on the reins.*

Figure 39 Allowed Stop from the Ground: When your horse yields to the rein, drop the reins on his neck, give him a pat, and step back for a moment. This is a form of the allowed stop, the immediate reward first discussed in Chapter 4.

Figure 40 **Staying Soft: After a while the horse should remain soft with light contact on the outside rein while the contact on the inside rein is dropped.**

As the horse begins to understand that he can avoid the unpleasant contact by lowering his head, he will begin to lower it as soon as you pick up the left rein. He is starting to understand how to soften and accept the contact correctly.

The first few times he softens as you are picking up the reins, immediately drop them on his neck, give him another pat and rest. When you're sure he does understand he should soften to the contact, you may begin to lower his head more and more by holding the inside rein up until he completely relaxes his poll and jaw. As the exercise is repeated, you will notice that the horse relaxes even more quickly. In fact, within a few minutes the horse will completely soften in his jaw, poll, and upper neck as soon as he feels the reins being picked up and before you even have a chance to establish contact. This is really wonderful when it happens because it means he has gone through the process of trial and error and figured out what you want.

If the horse begins to stiffen against the contact before you have a chance to reward him, play with the inside rein until he softens again and then reward immediately.

Staying Soft

This next exercise, *Staying Soft,* should be taught to the horse from both sides. When he shows an understanding of the concept of softening to initial contact, you may ask him to maintain softness. Now instead of dropping both reins on the horse's neck when he softens, keep a light contact on the outside rein and drop the contact (not the rein) on the inside (fig. 40). When the horse has maintained softness for a few seconds, reward him by dropping both reins and allow him to just stand there for a few moments. If the horse begins to stiffen against the contact before you have a chance to reward him, play with the inside rein until he softens again and then reward immediately.

Over Bending

By now, the horse is softening in the jaw, poll, and upper neck in response to contact with the reins only. The next exercise, *Over Bending,* is to teach him to soften at the base of his neck, and the easiest way to accomplish this is to gradually ask him to soften with more and more bend in the neck. This is shown in figure 41.

Releasing Muscle Knots

At this point in the exercises, you may have to change tactics for a bit and do a little physical therapy. Many horses, especially those that have been

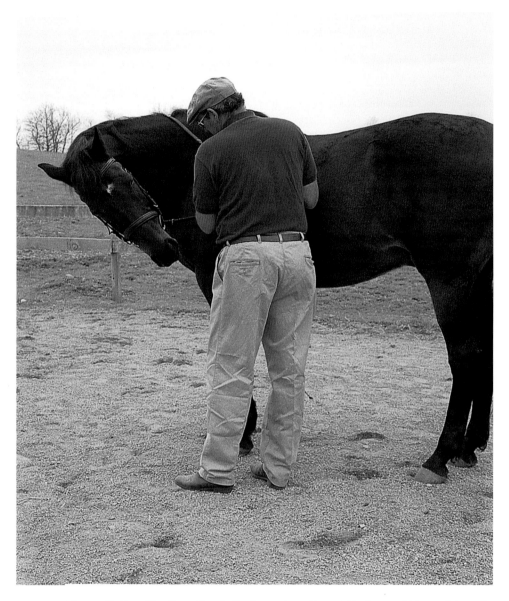

Figure 41 **Over Bending:** *Teach the horse to soften at the base of his neck by asking him to flex with more and more lateral bend.*

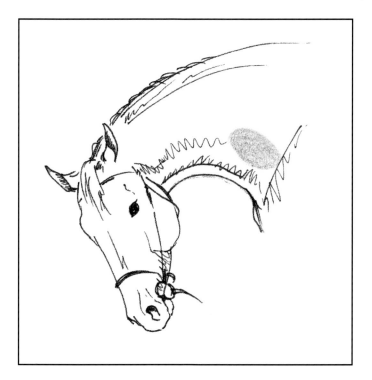

Figure 42 Many horses develop chronic muscles spasms in the area at the base of their neck (shown as the shaded spot in this drawing).

using their muscles incorrectly for a few years, develop chronic muscle spasms in the base of their necks. The shaded area of figure 42 shows the general location of these spasms.

A horse with muscle spasms in his neck has a sore, stiff neck. Just as you couldn't perform well with a stiff neck, neither can your horse. In order to have a soft, forward-going horse, you're going to have to fix this.

If you press your fingers into this area on a horse whose muscles are in spasm, it will feel like a piece of steel instead of a relaxed muscle. (A relaxed muscle should feel much like a piece of raw steak.) In order for the horse to become loose in his body, this muscle is going to have to be released. The way to release the muscle is to have him soften and bend as just described, and then, while he's still soft (well, as soft as a horse with a muscle spasm can get!) knead that area as though it were bread dough. Using your fingers (knuckles, thumb, whatever seems to work best), press into the muscle and massage it.

At first your horse may be a little sensitive and back away from the pressure you apply, but in just a few minutes he's going to realize that what you're doing feels very good, get a dreamy look in his eye, and start to move into your hand. When this happens let him "tell" you what feels best (fig. 43). If he starts to back away, lighten up, if he moves into you, press back into him until you are both using equal pressure.

If you work on this muscle for five or ten minutes a day for a few days, the muscle will change from feeling like a solid steel plate to feeling as though it consists of cords or ropes. The cords in the lighter breeds such as Quarter Horses, Thoroughbreds and Arabs tend to feel as though they are the diameter of your little finger, perhaps a quarter inch or so. The cords in the heavier horses feel larger, perhaps one-half inch in diameter.

If you continue massaging your horse in this area a few more days, the cords or ropes will break up into individual muscle knots. With the lighter breeds these feel to be about the size of acorns, with the larger breeds they can feel as large as walnuts. If you maintain the massage sessions, even these will soon disappear.

Because releasing the spasms in these muscles requires a minimum of several days (I have worked with some horses that took several weeks) you can continue with the training, but make a point of massaging your horse everyday until these muscles are completely released.

Softening the Horse's Body

After the horse is soft and responsive to the hand, it's time to teach him to soften in his body. Just as we had to teach the horse the correct response to contact with the bit in order to teach him to soften in his jaw, poll, and neck, we need to teach him to move away from the rider's leg in order to get him to understand that he should soften in his body. Of course, since we are working from the ground the rider's leg is simulated by use of the whip, or perhaps light taps of the hand.

The horse will learn to soften in his body when you teach him to bring his inside hind leg forward and under so that he places it down in front of the outside hind foot. This encourages him to bend because this is the easiest way for him to step up underneath his body and over with his inside hind leg. Our goal is to teach the horse to soften in his body in response to this aid, so as much bend as he offers should be gratefully accepted. There is no need for the horse to keep his forelegs in place. As long as he stays soft in

Figure 43 Feel around this area of the neck until you find the muscle knots, then experiment to find out what your horse likes best. Some prefer it when you make a fist and lean into them until they lean back. Others just prefer pressure from your fingers. In this picture, I'm keeping a very light contact on both reins as I rub this horse's neck.

*Figure 44 **For some work-in-hand it helps to bridge the reins in one hand, as shown. Using this method you can vary the pressure on the right, or left, rein individually.***

hand and moves softly away from light touches of the whip, the essential elements of the exercise are being accomplished.

To teach the horse this movement, ask him to soften as you have been doing. The amount of bend in the neck is not particularly important; whatever he offers is fine. Position your body so that you are facing his shoulder and looking directly over his withers (or imagine looking directly through his withers if it is above your line of sight).

Bridge both reins in the left hand by bringing the right rein over the top of the hand (between thumb and first finger), and the left rein around the bottom of the hand (fig. 44). Holding the reins this way allows you to feel the horse on each rein and vary the contact of either.

Now touch him lightly with the whip either at the hock or just above it. Many horses will kick out in response to the whip. Do not punish the horse for this. Ignore it, and ask him to move away from the whip again until he either moves away or steps up with the leg being tapped.

Within moments, the horse will either begin to step away by crossing his inside hind in front of his outside or he will try to move forward in response to the whip. If he offers a lateral step and crosses over—drop the reins and reward him. If he tries to go forward by running through the hand, resist the forward motion with the reins and ask again until he takes a lateral step.

Our goal is to teach the horse to soften in his body in response to an aid, so as much bend as he offers should be gratefully accepted.

Reward him for any motion where he brings his inside hind under himself and toward his outside hind, no matter how small. Repeat this procedure until he crosses his inside hind in front of the outside hind at the slightest touch of the whip and with a gentle resistance on the reins.

Often, horses will move away from the whip by stepping away with their outside hind first and then moving the inside hind so that it is next to the outside again. Moving from the whip (or rider's leg if under saddle) in this fashion has no relaxing effect. Indeed, a horse moving laterally by stepping away with the outside hind first and then "catching up" with the inside hind is falling out rather than engaging. Falling out is a sign of stiffness—not relaxation.

Most horses that "fall out" instead of stepping over will begin to step over after a few moments if you simply continue to ask him to move away and then reward the slightest attempt on his part to move his inside hind in front of the outside hind (fig. 45). However, I've run into a few horses that really didn't get the idea of stepping over until I proceeded on to the next exercise, moving his shoulders away.

Move Shoulders and Quarters

In this exercise, we ask the horse to move his quarters and shoulders laterally away from us. This is quite a lot to ask because he has to deal with crossing both the inside hind and front legs in front of the outside legs.

Figure 45 *Moving Your Horse's Hindquarters Away: In this photo I'm asking Bart to bring his inside hind leg forward and over so that he places it down in front of his outside hind foot. I have both reins "bridged" in my left hand and just enough contact on the outside rein so that Bart is quite happy to bend into it as he reaches for the bit. I began this movement by touching him near the hock with the whip, which I'm holding in my right hand. This exercise teaches him to move away from the rider's leg and, even more importantly, that the easiest way to move laterally is to bend throughout his body.*

In this example, he'll move to the right while bent to the left. Once again, we don't care about the amount of bend or whether the horse is bent evenly. We are simply trying to get the horse to cross his inside hind and forelegs in front of his outside legs. The amount of bend he finds it easiest to do it with is fine.

This movement can be fairly difficult for some horses to do at first. They seem to have trouble understanding that to perform it, they have to displace their shoulders to the outside of the bend. This means they have to shift their weight to the outside foreleg so the inside fore can come up and over.

Start by requesting only that the inside hind move over as in the preceding exercise. Then ask him to move his shoulders away too (fig. 46). Ideally, the way to ask him to move his shoulders is with the whip used near the girth in the area where your leg will be and with your inside hand putting a slight upward pressure on the corner of his mouth. If you are facing his shoulder and simply start to walk into him, he should begin to move over. However, until he understands what is expected, it is helpful to touch him, or even give him a gentle push on the inside shoulder. Sometimes you may have to bump him lightly with your hip near the girth. I have worked with horses that found this movement so difficult I literally had to pick up their inside front foot and move it over for them several times before they caught on. So be patient. If the horse doesn't catch on easily, it's because he doesn't know how to move his weight and shoulder over. He's not resistant—just a bit clumsy.

The Natural Circle in Hand

As the horse begins to understand the concept of displacing his shoulder and moving his whole body sideways, it is possible to ask him to move away from the inside leg (whip) and into your outside hand. The tools available for this are the softness gained in the above exercises and his Natural Circle.

This exercise gives him the idea of bending and moving from the inside leg to the outside hand as he walks on a circle. It also teaches him to move forward with a small angle to the line of travel. This is really quite a large issue in training. As you may recall from Chapter 12, *Developing Working Gaits*, knowing how to balance bend, forward and lateral motion is an essential element in teaching the horse to carry a rider properly.

Working the horse in hand on his Natural Circle will also give him a chance to feel the same balance of bend, forward, and lateral motion you felt while walking on your circle, although he probably won't feel the same looseness you felt on your circle for a while yet.

Start the exercise by asking him to move his quarters over and follow immediately by asking him to move his shoulders away as described above and as shown in figure 47A and B. After moving him over like this for a few steps, you can allow the horse to walk a little more forward while keeping some of the lateral movement. To do this, simply turn your body a bit so that instead of walking directly into his shoulder you are walking diagonally—

147

Figure 46 Moving the Whole Horse Away: I am asking the horse to move his shoulders and quarters away by touching him with the whip near the girth area; putting a slight upward pressure on the corner of his mouth with the inside rein; and maintaining a contact on the outside rein. This horse is moving easily away so I'm just following along; however, with another horse you might need to give a gentle push on the inside shoulder until he begins to understand what is expected. I like the way this horse is over bending and "wrapping himself around me" as he reaches to the outside rein because I want him to learn it is easier to move when he bends.

more toward his neck than toward his shoulder. This should put the horse on a circle moving at an angle to his line as shown in figure 47C. As you move onto the circle, take the reins in both hands, left rein in your left hand, right rein in your right. Hold them as you would normally for riding.

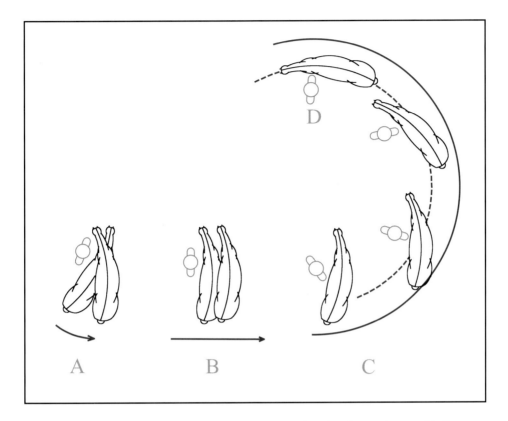

Figure 47 *Directing the Horse on to His Natural Circle: This figure shows a bird's eye view of the exercises shown in photos 45, 46 and 48. In A, the handler is asking the horse to move just his quarters away by touching the hock with the whip while looking toward the horse's withers. B shows the handler—still looking toward the withers—touching the horse behind the girth to ask him to move his quarters and shoulders away. C shows the handler guiding the horse on to his Natural Circle with some angle to the line of travel by turning his body toward (as though looking through) the horse's neck. Finally, D shows the horse has no angle at all when the handler looks straight ahead.*

You can increase the amount of angle the horse has to his line of travel by turning your body more toward his withers, and decrease it by turning yourself more toward his front end (fig. 47D). By experimenting a little with the size of the circle and the amount of the horse's angle, you will be able to find his Natural Circle.

If you recall from Chapter 16, *Your Horse's Natural Circle,* the horse's Natural Circle is unique to every horse at every gait so I can't tell you precisely what size circle to walk on. However, there are some guidelines to go by. Your horse's Natural Circle will be a little smaller than a circle he can bend to match the circumference of and just walk on. His Natural Circle will be small enough so that he needs to move on a small angle to his line of travel.

A large, long-backed horse will have a bigger Natural Circle than a small horse or one with a shorter back.

When you find the circle on which it is easiest to keep the horse walking forward with a little bend and angle to his line, the horse is on his Natural Circle.

Just as you could feel your Natural Circle, you will be able to feel your horse's Natural Circle. When he is on his Natural Circle, you'll find it easy to keep him moving softly around. If the circle is too small, he'll want to move on too much of an angle to his line and it will be difficult to keep him going forward. If the circle is too big, he will lose the bend and want to walk through your hands on a straight line. It's entirely fitting and proper to experiment a little and try making the circle bigger or smaller. When you find the circle on which it is easiest to keep the horse walking forward with a little bend and angle to his line, the horse is on his Natural Circle.

Once the horse has the idea of walking on his Natural Circle, you (or the horse!) may want try it at a very slow trot, almost a Western jog (fig. 48). The reins are still held in two hands but keep them a bit longer so you're a little further from him. I'm often surprised that people who would appear just a little too small to be trotting their horses in hand are able to do it rather well. However, this exercise at the trot is not mandatory, and it is perfectly acceptable to go onto the longe at this point.

Work on the Longe Line

Now that the horse knows how to soften, bend, and move into the outside rein, it is possible to begin correct work on the longe line. As I mentioned in Chapter 17, *First Touch,* for a horse to be longeing properly, he has to be soft, bending, and relaxed.

Because work on the longe is simply a continuation of the work in hand, we can have the horse bend, move slightly laterally, and stay in balance on his Natural Circle. Like work in hand, work on the longe has the advantage that the horse still doesn't have to deal with our weight. An additional benefit of correct work on the longe line is that the size of the circle can be

Figure 48 *This horse has found his Natural Circle at the trot. He's stretching over his topline and his outside ribcage, as he reaches into the outside rein. He is nicely engaged, swinging his legs freely, and keeping a wonderfully consistent tempo. I'm holding the right rein and the whip in my right hand, which is just visible below my right elbow. I'm walking toward a point just behind his poll, as he moves at a slight angle to his line of travel.*

increased enough for the horse to begin to swing his legs freely and develop his muscles correctly.

As the horse finds his balance on the larger circle and begins swinging his legs, he discovers that moving correctly feels good and that is the *reward of the exercise.* (Reward of the exercise was first mentioned in Chapter 4, and refers to the fact that correct performance feels good to a horse and is reward-ing in and of itself.) This is a great opportunity to show the horse reward of the exercise.

As previously mentioned, work on the longe line is also a way of deal-ing with horses that have too much energy or need some time to settle down. So the amount of time spent on the longe each day, and the total number of days you just longe your horse or longe him before rid-ing depends entirely on the horse you have. However, we also have to consider that allowing your horse to longe incorrectly after doing the work in hand would be con-fusing for him. He wouldn't know what it is you really wanted from him—should he go in balance and rhythm or just run around? To avoid confusing the horse and to set definite limits that he can understand, allow him to "get the bucks out" for a few minutes when first taken to the ring. Then it is time to settle down. Once he has had his chance to blow off some steam and you begin work, he is expected to always go softly in balance and rhythm. Rule Number 3, *Every Step Counts*, is in full force!

As the horse finds his balance on the larger circle and begins swinging his legs, he discovers that moving correctly feels good.

The longe line itself should be the same type as used in the early leading exercises. It is best if made from wide, soft cotton web and run through the inside bit ring, over the poll, and then to the outside bit ring. Arranged this way, the longe only puts pressure on the corners of the mouth and the poll, not on the bars of the mouth.

The best side reins are made of leather and have a rubber doughnut in them. Side reins that are made with long elastic pieces in them have too much give and encourage the horse to take too much contact, which often leads to pulling. Side reins with lots of Dee rings on them to adjust the length tend to be too heavy for the thickness of material and are too floppy, which discour-ages the horse from taking any contact. Horses find them annoying. If you don't have side reins you can make do with baling twine tied in safety knots around the saddle billet and bit ring.

Before attaching the side reins, it is a good idea to ask the horse to soft-en to the bit using the longe line as you would the inside rein. Lift the longe line so it puts an upward pressure on the inside ring of the bit just as you did with the inside rein when working him in hand. The horse should readily accept this and soften to it.

The side reins should be adjusted so that they are both of equal length. They should be long enough that the horse is just touching the bit when he

Figure 49 Adjusting the Side Reins: These side reins are both the same length and the horse is reaching into a comfortable contact on the outside rein. As he bends, the inside rein becomes loose—a sure sign the horse is bending correctly by stretching his outside rib cage.

is soft and relaxed in the jaw, poll, and neck (fig. 49). To be very clear about this point, the side reins should not be holding the horse's nose in. He should be reaching out a little to the bit from the relaxed, soft position he was in when doing the early in-hand exercises. If the horse is pulling on the side reins, they are too short and should be lengthened. When they are adjusted correctly, the inside rein will become slack as the horse bends.

Beginning to Longe

Once the horse is outfitted with the longe line and side reins, keep the longe coiled in one hand and hold the end near the horse in the other so that you can stand as close to him as you did when holding the reins. Generally, I'll begin work on the longe so close to the horse that I'm still using the dressage whip and will not use the longe whip for several minutes. Now go through the same sequence of exercises as described earlier in this chapter: ask the horse to move his quarters away from you, then his shoulders, and then move him out to his Natural Circle. The difference this time is that you are using the longe line to vary the contact on the inside of the bit, and contact on the outside of the bit is being made by the side rein.

When the horse is walking calmly around on the circle, move about four or five feet away from him toward the center of the circle. Do this slowly and maintain contact by letting the longe line "draw" through your hand as you go. (However, be very careful not to let the longe line get wrapped around your hand!)

Now you may ask the horse to trot off slowly. In most cases, you will have to walk with him on a small circle at first (fig. 50A). As the horse settles into his trot, you can let him spiral out to a larger circle as you move closer to the center of the circle by allowing the horse to draw the longe line through some more (fig. 50B).

The horse will begin to go too fast or lose his bend occasionally as he explores the limits of his balance (Chapter 3, *Learning*). When he does, you can help him re-establish his balance by walking out to the horse, shortening the longe line as you go (fig. 50C). Walking out to him and shortening the longe line puts the horse on a smaller circle so you can touch him with the whip near his quarters and increase the contact on the inside by raising your inside hand. The actions of touching him with the whip and raising your hand are the same aids used during work in hand to teach him to soften to the hand and to bend away from your leg. In addition, we know from Chapter 12, *Developing Working Gaits* that bringing a horse to a smaller circle reminds him it's easier to move on a small circle when he softens and relaxes than when he remains stiff or rigid. Everything about this correction leads the horse to the conclusion that he should soften and bend as the circle gets smaller.

We also know from Chapter 16, *Your Horse's Natural Circle* that it may be easier on the horse to correct him on the small circle than to let him go incorrectly on the large circle, but it still isn't "easy." What is easiest for a horse on the longe is to go around on a larger circle bending and in balance. So as soon as the horse softens, allow him to move onto a larger circle by letting him draw the longe line through your hand.

Most horses will figure out very quickly that the size of the circle decreases when they get stiff and increases as soon as they soften. They also

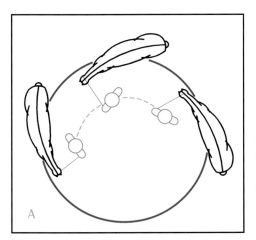

Expanding the Circle on the Longe.
(Figures 50 A, B, and C).

Figures 50 A and B Stay about four
or five feet from your horse as he is
trotting slowly on a small circle (A).
Then you can let him spiral out to
a larger circle as you move closer to
the center, by allowing him to draw
out the longe line (B).

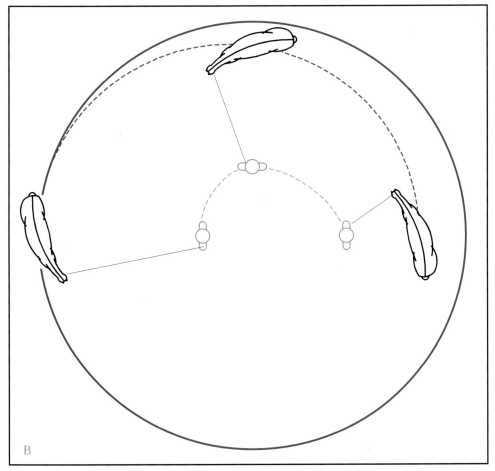

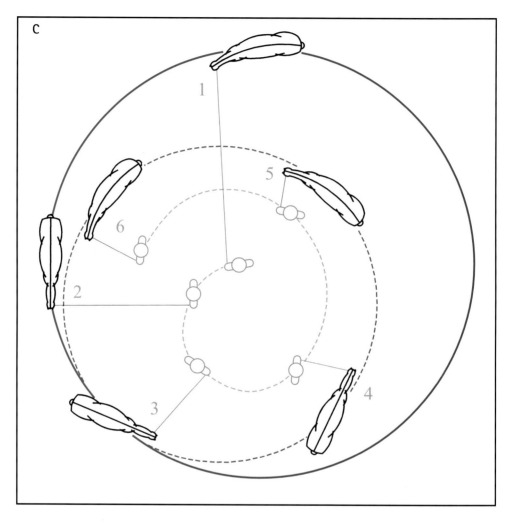

Figure 50 C **You can help your horse find his balance again by leading him back to the small circle. Do this by walking out to him, shortening the longe line as you go.**

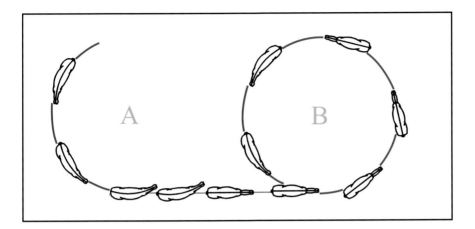

Figure 51 Teaching Balance While on a Straight Line: Because a horse is more likely to be balanced on a circle than on a straight line, lead him on to a circle anytime you need to rebalance him.

realize that the contact remains soft and inviting when they stay soft and the contact becomes mildly unpleasant when they begin to stiffen. You'll know when your horse understands this because he will begin to soften and bend again as soon as he feels the contact increase. Soon, the horse will become so accustomed to this that by merely raising the longe line a little and taking a step or two toward him, he will realize that he should soften again. When he does soften, relax the contact and continue on. The horse is becoming sensitive to the aids and is learning to always soften to them.

Whenever the horse moves on to a larger circle, he is, by default, moving into the outside rein. As he learns to stay soft and move to the outside rein, he learns his job is rather pleasant and much easier than stiffening against the aids. As the horse becomes accustomed to going around in balance and to staying relaxed, you can move to the center of the circle and replace the dressage whip with the longe whip.

In time, you can teach your horse to keep the same balance he's developed on the circle while he's traveling on a straight line. When he has a nice bend, angle and tempo, lead him off the circle and on to a line (fig. 51A). If at first he loses his bend or rhythm while moving down the long side, guide him back to a smaller circle and reestablish the balance (B). As the horse gets better at this, you will be able to keep him balanced on the straight line for a longer distance.

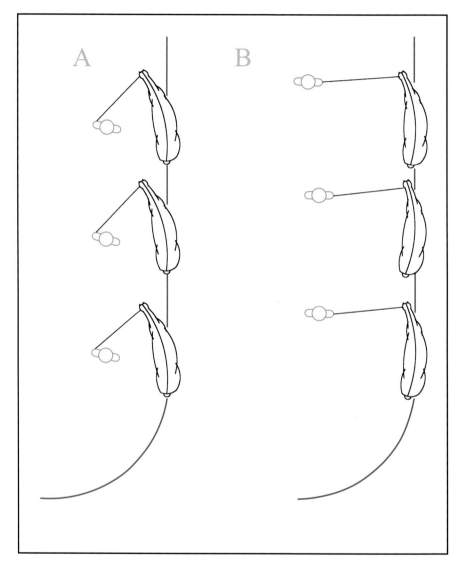

Figure 52 *You can teach your horse to do a shoulder-in while on the longe line by staying next to him and behind his shoulder as you lead him off the circle and down the long side (A). To allow him to lengthen his stride on the long side, position yourself more toward his head as you take him off the circle (B).*

Once your horse has become fairly good at keeping his bend and balance on the long side, you can have a little fun with him on the longe while teaching him two dressage movements—a shoulder-in, and a lengthening. Walk out to the horse (shortening the line as you go) and walk him down the long side. If you stay close to him and parallel to his shoulder, he will move down the long side at an angle to the line of travel with an even bend—a shoulder-in (fig. 52A). If you make the longe line longer and move a little ahead of his shoulder, he will tend to go on the line and lengthen his stride—a lengthening (fig. 52B).

Working horses from the ground is safe, incredibly effective, and a lot of fun.

The work in hand and on the longe is absolutely necessary to the process of training. Although it may feel a bit awkward at first, taking the time to become comfortable with these skills will pay dividends throughout the horse's career—and yours. Working horses from the ground this way is safe, incredibly effective, and a lot of fun.

19 Under Saddle, and on to the Aids

The purpose of the early work under saddle is to show the horse that the work done in hand and on the longe line carries through under saddle. The horse continues to soften to the hand, move away from the rider's leg, and to walk and trot on his Natural Circle, but now with the rider's added weight. Using the seat, and outside leg, as aids will also be taught in these early sessions.

To begin, bring your horse to the ring in saddle and bridle with the longe line attached. Work him in hand and on the longe line as described in the previous chapters, and when you think he's ready, it's time to mount.

It's not necessary to use an assistant if you're re-schooling a horse that's already been broken to saddle; however, if you do, your horse may find it easier to understand he's doing the same thing now with a rider on his back that he had just been doing without one. The assistant's first function is just to be live weight; his only responsibility is to grab mane if necessary. Your job as the ground person is to keep the horse's attention and be the active instruction giver. When the horse is first mounted, you should stay close and run through the exercises already taught as though the rider isn't there. After the horse has become used to a rider on his back, start to have the assistant give the aids from the saddle.

To teach the horse to accept aids from the rider instead of the ground person, have the rider use an aid, and then, if the horse doesn't understand, ask him from the ground in the way he is accustomed. Working this way, the horse will quickly begin to accept the aids given by the rider. As he does, move further away and let the rider take over.

Soften From the Saddle

Whether you've used an assistant or not, eventually you will find yourself mounted on your horse. Once up and settled, ask the horse to soften to the hands the same way you did in the first in-hand exercises. Raise one rein while keeping a light contact on the other. The horse should bend a little into the direction of the raised hand (which makes that the inside hand), but the rein in the other hand will prevent him from bending too much. As soon as the horse softens the slightest amount, drop the reins and pat him.

If the horse begins to back up, or stiffen, instead of softening to the rein, create more bend in the neck with the hitchhiker rein (see p. 74). Remember as you ask him to bend with the inside rein, the contact on the outside rein must be soft enough so that it allows the horse to bend. If your horse does not soften in his jaw, poll, and neck, the ground person needs to step in or you need to dismount and review the groundwork. It's important to stay with this exercise until he softens as soon as you pick up the reins.

More Bend

Next, following the pattern of exercises done in hand, ask for more lateral bend in the horse's neck. Do this by bringing the inside rein up and away from the horse while keeping a light contact on the outside rein (fig. 53). The point of the exercise is to show the horse that he should relax and soften to the bit, not simply allow you to pull his head around. You'll know your horse is relaxing his muscles and accepting the bit correctly if he stays bent to the inside and keeps a soft contact on the outside rein when you drop the inside rein.

Moving the Quarters

When the horse understands that he should soften to the rider's hand, it is time to ask him to move his quarters away from your leg. Start by asking him to soften to the hand with just a little bend in his neck. As he softens to the

Figure 53 *Ask for more bend in the horse's neck by bringing the inside rein up and away from the horse while keeping a light contact on the outside rein.*

contact, move your inside hand a little away from the horse with an opening rein. As you do this, turn your upper body so that your belly button is pointed toward his inside shoulder, and touch him lightly with your inside leg. Your outside leg is passive and may actually have to be taken away from a very green horse. The horse should move his quarters by bringing his inside hind leg over just as he did during the in-hand exercise.

If he doesn't move, try increasing the bend in his neck by raising your inside hand a little more and touch him lightly with the whip as you did when working him from the ground (fig. 54). If he still doesn't move, get off and move him over from the ground a few times, then remount and ask from the saddle again.

If your horse walks straight ahead instead of swinging his quarters out, give and take on the outside rein to stop him. Keep asking until he does take a lateral step and then reward. Repeat this exercise until your horse moves lightly away in response to light touches of your hand and leg.

Moving the Shoulder

When he moves his quarters easily, you can ask him to move his shoulders over too. Begin by having him step away with his quarters for a step or two. Then, raise your inside hand so it is a mild hitchhiker rein and open the outside rein about an inch or so. Your upper body should be pointed straight ahead, or very slightly toward the horse's outside shoulder. Now, as you lightly touch him with your inside leg, give and take a little with the outside hand too. Again, repeat this until the horse moves over from light touches.

Finding the Natural Circle While Mounted

As shown in figure 55A and B, when the horse moves his quarters and shoulders away from the leg, he will be moving at an angle to his line. Typically, a green horse will only walk at an angle to his line for a few steps before losing the angle. Then it is necessary to stop and readjust by asking him to just move his quarters for a step or two (fig. 55C), and then immediately ask him to move his shoulders too, so that he's moving at an angle to his line for a few steps.

In a little time, you will be able to smooth out the aids used to regain your angle when he loses it. Then you won't have to actually stop, just begin to stop, and as you do, begin moving the quarters and the shoulders over again. At this point, you're walking on the circle with an angle to the circumference (fig. 55D and E), making adjustments as you go. Of course, as

Figure 54 To help your horse understand that he should move away from your leg, try increasing the bend in his neck by raising your inside hand as you touch him lightly with the whip behind your leg. These are the same "aids" you use when working him from the ground, so if he doesn't figure it out in a few minutes, he is telling you that you haven't taught him the in-hand lessons well enough.

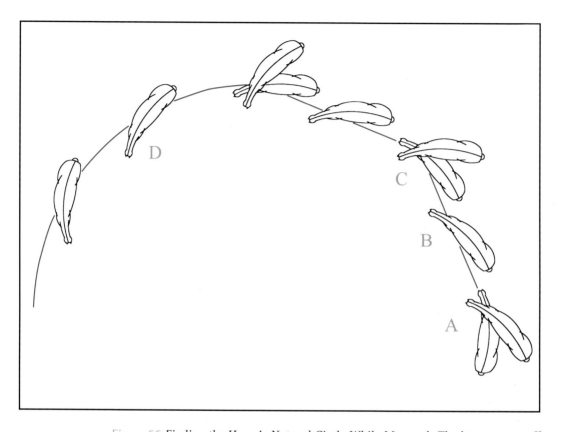

Figure 55 **Finding the Horse's Natural Circle While Mounted: The horse starts off with a slight bend and is then asked to move over—first his quarters, then his quarters and shoulders (A). A horse just learning to bend and move at an angle to his line will not be able to continue moving this way for long, so you have to stop, reorganize, and again ask him move his quarters, and then his shoulders and quarters over (C). After a while it won't be necessary to stop and reorganize (D).**

with all the early exercises, the exact amount of bend and angle of travel will be determined by what the horse finds easiest.

It is not all that unusual for a horse, already well schooled from the ground, to walk on a circle with a good bend and angle to the line (fig. 56) before you're ready to ask him. If he does, that's fine; it means you've done a good job with the groundwork, so reward him with an allowed stop,

Figure 56 *When a horse begins to walk easily, keeping a soft bend and an angle to his line, he is being ridden on his Natural Circle.*

which is done the same way mounted as from the ground. Drop the reins on the horse's neck and give him a pat.

It's most likely that when the horse begins to walk easily on a circle while keeping a soft bend and an angle to the line, he is on his Natural Circle. As he settles and discovers how easy it is to move this way, you'll find he begins to relax and take longer, looser strides.

After going through these exercises a few times, the horse will probably begin to go from halt to walking on the circle in a single step or two. At that point he may decide to try moving this way in the trot on his own. If he does, great! Let him go for a short period and then reward. If the horse doesn't offer the trot on his own, ask him by clicking your tongue, touching him with your legs, or even tapping him very lightly with the whip. If he trots, fine; let him go for a long enough period so that he understands that this is what you wanted, and then reward with an allowed stop.

There will be some horses that don't want to break into the trot. That's fine too. They are nervous about having weight on their backs and require a little more time at the walk until comfortable enough to trot. Remember, the goal isn't just to make the horse trot, the goal is to teach the horse to relax and trot easily so that he enjoys carrying the rider.

Remember, the goal isn't just to make the horse trot, the goal is to teach the horse to relax and trot easily so that he enjoys carrying the rider.

20

Falling In and Out

*O*nce the horse begins to trot on his circle, it won't take him long to start exploring the limits of his balance. When he does, he'll go beyond these limits, and lose his balance.

At first (maybe in the first few days, maybe in the first week or two—you have to decide), you're going to have to gently bring him back to the walk or halt, reorganize, and begin again as described in the previous chapter. But soon, you will want to try and restore his balance while still in the trot.

The trot is uniquely suited to teaching the horse to deal with balance. It has just enough speed and momentum to give the horse incentive to stay balanced but not so much as to make it impossible to restore it if lost. The walk is too easy for a horse to do incorrectly—it provides no incentive. The canter has too much momentum and speed; it's too difficult for a horse just learning to carry a rider correctly to restore balance in it.

When dealing with a horse falling in or out, you have to recognize the problem: he has lost his balance. The symptom will be the circle getting larger or smaller. In this

The trot is uniquely suited to teaching the horse to deal with balance.

situation, leaning on a rein and speeding up are also symptoms, not problems in themselves.

If you try to correct the symptoms instead of the problem, you only have two options. One is to use the whip or leg and spur aggressively. This approach will get a horse to move in or out away from your leg, but only after he has gone through a process of trial and error to figure out what is expected. It's likely to be a fairly random process too, one that may well include bucking, rearing, kicking, and bolting. Eventually, he will get around to moving away from the leg, but it is going to be a long time before he moves from it loosely, softly, and with trust in his rider.

When dealing with a horse falling in and out, you have to recognize the problem: he has lost his balance.

Another way of dealing with the symptoms of falling in or out is trying to hold him on a circle with the rein. With this approach, the symptom of a horse leaning on the rein soon becomes a problem unto itself. Keeping the circle from getting smaller by holding the horse out with the inside rein will only worsen the situation as the horse and rider each get stiff and sore from all that pulling and leaning.

So the real problem of a horse falling in or out, is he's lost his balance. The actual falling in or out, the leaning on one rein or the other and the feeling of him being against your leg are symptoms of the problem.

Now, remember from Chapter 12, *Developing Working Gaits* that it's a lot easier for your horse to carry you correctly than for him to carry you while he's out of balance. This simple fact makes your life much less complicated. You don't need to try and force or coerce your horse into doing the easier thing—just set him up so that he can figure it out for himself.

In order to set a horse up so he can figure these things out for himself, you have to be a little clever with your aids. You need to be clever because you're only going to suggest to him that he does the right thing, while allowing him to do the wrong thing until he figures it out for himself. Well, perhaps this is a lesson best learned by example.

Falling Out

In figure 57A, the horse is moving along on a circle. By point B, he has started to fall out. When your horse is falling out, turn your upper body in so that your belly button is pointed to the center of the circle and use a hitchhiker on the inside rein strongly enough to bring his nose around until it is point-

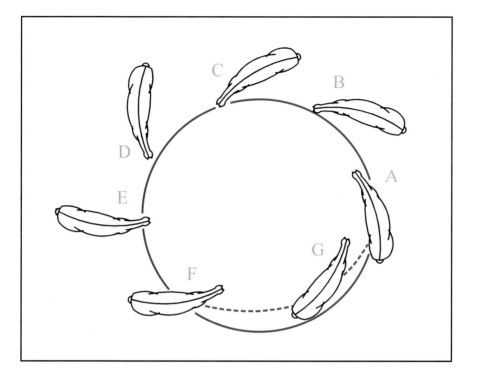

Figure 57 *Falling Out: Rather than fight with your horse if he's falling out, just keep his nose pointed toward the center of the circle (B to E), until he realizes it's much easier to listen to your aids (F to A).*

ed at the center of the circle too. By pointing your belly button and his nose to the center of the circle, he will start to swing his quarters out (fig. 57C). Within a few strides, he'll find himself going around the circle almost perpendicular to the circumference (fig. 57D).

Now here's the part that requires a little cleverness with the aids. The whole time you're bringing him around with your seat and hitchhiker rein, you have to gently give and take the outside rein, touch him lightly with your outside leg, and ask him to move straight ahead instead of falling out.

You see it's a little sneaky isn't it? The hitchhiker and seat are not preventing him from falling out at all; in fact, they'll contribute to it if used too strongly. So we're not helping him, we're letting him get himself into a bit of a pickle and then have to find his own way out.

Of course we really can't help all that much as we haven't used the outside leg as an aid yet so he doesn't even know to move away from it. But rather than getting aggressive with our aids and forcing him to move from it, we're going to use falling out as an opportunity to explain the outside leg to him. To see how this works, let's continue with the example.

By the time you've arrived at point D, he is falling out as much as any horse can, but because you've brought his nose around and pointed your seat in the right direction, he's falling out onto the circumference of the circle he started out on. So, by the time he arrives at E, he has begun to realize that falling out is not nearly as much fun as he had thought it would be, and he is also still going around on the same circle. What's more, he is going around it in the most difficult way possible.

As horses are very rational creatures, he is going to start to look for a way to make his life easier. What do you suppose he finds but your outside aids asking him to go straight ahead. So he does. He will cut right through the circle beginning at F, and by point G you need to start asking him to move out again. By now he realizes that listening to your aids has made his life easier, so by point A you can reestablish the circle with correct bend and angle to the line. Go a few more strides, drop the reins and reward him.

The above example is fairly ideal, and realistically it will probably take several times around the circle before the horse begins to follow the outside aids. Also, it's almost a certainty that you will have to deal with him falling out several more times until the outside aids are fully established. There are, however, some larger issues to be learned from this process.

As this method of dealing with falling out allows the horse to learn for himself, he learns to listen to aids, not run from them. He's encouraged to stay soft because he finds that yielding to the aids is easier than fighting them. In fact, he will pay close attention to those small light aids you give, realizing now they are there to help him. Not only did your aids assist him in finding a solution, they were always kind and considerate of him as well. After all, you were not telling him to fall out, but just going along with his idea while quietly suggesting that he go along with yours.

Falling In

It's possible to use a similar approach to deal with falling in. Again, you have to give your horse some experience at moving in balance before you use this approach and try to have him correct his balance while trotting. But, if he's

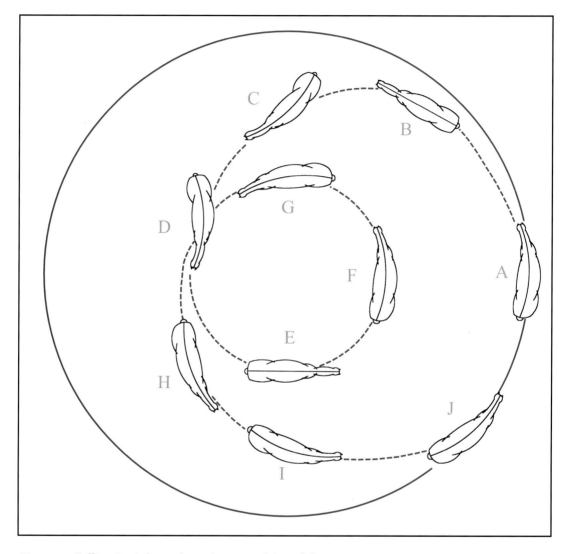

Figure 58 Falling In: When a horse begins to fall in (B), you can let him continue to fall in (C, D, and E), until he realizes you are not going to rescue him. As a result, he will decide on his own that he is better off, and more comfortable, moving on to a larger circle with the correct bend (F to J).

ready, when he begins to fall in, you have the option of just letting him fall in until he decides that he's better off moving on a larger circle. The basic procedure is to keep the same contact on the outside rein while slightly opening and raising the inside rein, which invites him to bend but also allows him to fall in to his heart's content. Your inside leg continues to ask politely for him to move out and away, but if he doesn't want to, well, he doesn't want to.

Remember the lesson learned— trust your horse when he says he needs a break.

This technique is illustrated in figure 58. As with the previous example of falling out, the figure shows the problem corrected in a single revolution, but in reality it will likely take several for the horse to figure this out. At point A everything is fine, but by point B he has lost his bend and begins to fall in. At C he's inverted his bend and is really falling in; he continues to do so until point D. Now he realizes that I am not coming to his rescue and if he doesn't stop falling in he may well fall down. So he corrects himself at points E and F, and I can then ask him to start moving out to the larger circle again at G, H, I, J. As moving on a large circle is easier for a horse than falling in onto a very small circle, most horses become quite agreeable in very little time.

Correcting his balance while trotting around carrying a rider is actually a pretty complex task for a horse. If your horse isn't really ready to be able to do it, he'll probably pick up more speed and start to get a little frantic when you ask him to try. If he does, just gently bring him back to the walk, let him calm down as you reassure him, and then using the exercises from the previous chapter, rebalance him and bring him back to the trot to try again. It's also possible that he'll bring himself back to the walk when he loses his balance. That is perfectly fine. He's just clever enough to know his limits.

Of course I can already hear the protests, "If you let him walk every time he loses his balance, he'll learn he can walk whenever he wants to!"

So? What's wrong with that? I let my horses walk when they want to and I don't think they want to walk nearly as much as I do. Remember the lesson learned in Rule Number 2, *Reward in Proportion*—trust your horse when he says he needs a break. And no, this is not off the topic of falling in and out— it goes to the heart of it.

Horses do not like being out of balance. You can use the opportunity of your horse learning to balance with you on his back to show him more than the mere mechanics of staying vertical—you can use it to show him that you're on his side and he can trust you. If you do, the rest of training, regardless of your particular goal, will be much easier.

21 Changing Bend and Direction

Changing bend and direction correctly goes well beyond merely riding across the diagonal—this little exercise changes everything! We use it to help our horses make the transition from balanced movement to balanced weight, to go from being over bent to being evenly bent, and from moving with an angle to the line of travel to moving on the line. Hidden in this simple, mundane and overlooked exercise, we find the secret to the dressage world's great enigma—just how do you "make your horse straight and drive him forward?"[1]

Trying to *make* unprepared horses "straight and forward" is mysterious because there is no direct way to *make* horses do either. As I explained back in Chapter 16 *Your Horse's Natural Circle,* we have no direct way of engaging, elevating, or evenly bending a horse. You cannot use your hands to lift him off his forehand and create elevation, nor can you use your legs

Now here, hidden in this simple, mundane, and overlooked little exercise—changing bend and direction—we find the secret to the dressage world's great mystery—just how do you "make your horse straight and drive him forward?"

---

4 *Gustav Steinbrecht's famous quote from* Gymnasium des Pferdes (1885), *is considered the foundation of dressage.*

to force engagement as both will interfere with free swinging movement. You cannot evenly bend a horse with your legs as they have no mechanical effect, and if you try to bend him with your hands, you interfere with the engagement of the hind legs. In large part this is why we've been allowing the horse to move with as much bend and angle to his line as he needed while he developed the strength and coordination to proceed.

Even with a horse properly prepared changing bend and direction is not simple. In fact, there is one method used for a greener horse and a second method for use with a horse as he gets stronger. The first method is used to help a horse maintain his balance of movement, while the second method helps to make the bend even and to balance the weight. Once the horse's weight is balanced and bend is even, the second method is used because it's the correct way to ride a balanced horse through a change of direction (although many horses will still warm up daily using the first method).

Both methods change the horse's bend before his direction (so he can maintain his balance) and both methods rely on a concept I call "releasing the bend." You release the bend by softening or giving the outside rein enough so that the horse begins to straighten and lengthen his body as he seeks the contact of that rein.

Horses need you to release the bend because they lengthen their frames as they change bend—a green horse considerably more than an advanced horse—but they both lengthen during the change. Advanced horses also use the "release" to help distinguish the "change-bend" aids from the aids for more bend, angle, engagement, or even different gaits.

The Aids

The correct aids to release and then change the bend are shown in figure 59. Point A shows the horse correctly moving into the outside hand. In order to change the bend, first release it by softening the outside hand while at the same time moving the outside leg forward (B). As the horse seeks out the missing contact, he begins to straighten throughout his body (C). Completing the process of change, the new inside hand and leg ask the horse to soften, bend, and move into the new outside hand, which accepts the energy and takes over the task of guiding the horse (D). Remember to keep the rhythm of your aids throughout the change. Your current outside rein is released by progressively softening it and taking it back less and less each stride. Don't just drop it. Your *new* inside leg slides forward to the girth and lightly taps the horse each stride—it doesn't come forward and grab him.

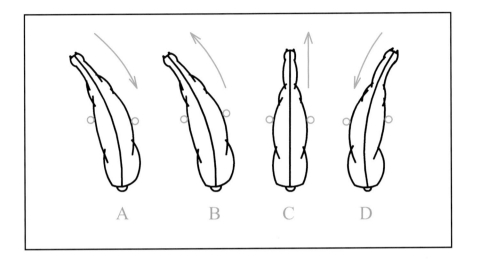

Figure 59 The arrows depict the action of the outside rein during a change of bend, and the small circles show the position of the rider's legs. At A, (before the change of bend begins) the right (outside) rein accepts the energy, and the right leg is back from the girth a small amount. At B, the rider softens the right rein—"releasing the bend"— and brings his right leg forward. At C, the rider brings his right (now inside) rein up in the hitchhiker position, at the same time using his right leg at the girth to request and encourage the horse to begin to bend in the new direction. At D, the rider draws back on the left (new outside) rein just enough to accept the energy and provide contact. He also slides his left leg back a small amount.

You may find it easier to change bend in the rising trot. By applying your aids as you rise and releasing them as you sit, you'll keep the rhythm and your timing will be perfect. Changing your posting diagonal at the beginning helps the green horse to understand that a change of rising diagonal is soon to be followed by a change of bend, which also gives him the idea he should be sensitive to changes in the seat generally.

When your horse is keeping his balance trotting on the circle in both directions it is time to introduce this exercise. At this point, the horse has balanced movement, but he still hasn't achieved balanced weight. You've been riding him at an angle to his line and letting him over bend to balance his movement. You should have the problems of falling in and out fairly well sorted out by now.

With a young horse the process is to change the bend and, after it is well established, follow the new bend into the new direction. The rider's primary concern must be to keep the horse moving in balance and softly into the outside aids. The exercise must be planned to allow as much time and room as necessary to attain this goal.

Figure 60 shows a typical exercise to introduce the horse to a correct change of direction. At point A, the horse is on the circle to the left, moving well into the outside hand. At point B, begin to release the existing bend by softening the right hand and bringing your right leg forward. At point C, the horse has straightened, so ask him to move away from your right leg and into your left hand. By D, you start a new bend. From D to E, coming off the diagonal and continuing on the long side for a while, ask for more bend and angle to the line. Keep the angle and bend until he is really secure in your aids and then, with light touches of your outside rein and leg, ask him to follow his new bend onto the new circle at F.

While going from D to E with that much angle and bend it feels almost, but not quite, like falling out. It's more of a drifting out. But the lessons on falling out in the previous chapter have taught your horse to respond to your light touches of outside leg and hand to guide him onto the new circle. It really does feel like following his bend into the new direction.

Yes, I know it's a tad strange to say that you should allow your horse to over bend, and drift out. And to make it worse, I'm not just allowing it I'm actually encouraging the horse to over bend and drift out. In fact, if he isn't over bending and moving out enough, I'm going to pick up the inside rein and throw those shoulders over just like I did in the ground exercises.

But don't worry about the horse over bending or falling out. You need a horse that's willing to do both to ride him on his line with no angle and an even bend while using only aids that request, encourage, and allow.

To understand why we need a horse that wants to over bend, stop for a moment and ask yourself just how it is you bend a horse? The answer is simple—*you* don't. *You* can't. Only the horse can bend the horse. The best *you* can do is put him on a circle that encourages him to bend. The worst you can do is to bend some of him by pulling on the inside rein (which is not the same as briefly lifting the inside rein to pop his shoulder over as a correction, which I suggested above).

What you can do though, is use your outside rein to prevent a horse who knows it's easier to bend from bending too much. *You* can't use your outside leg to prevent a horse who is out of balance from falling out, but you can use it to ask a horse who has learned to trust your aids and balance his movement to stop drifting out.

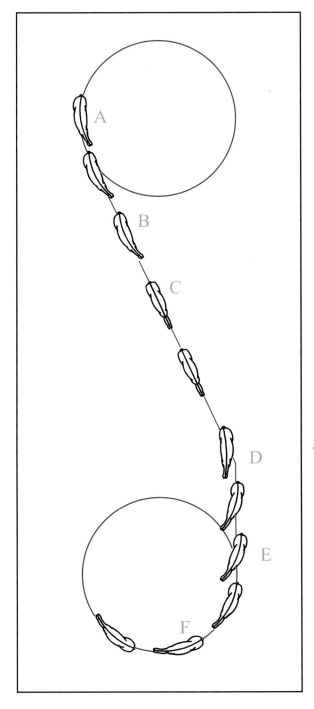

Figure 60 When changing bend and direction in the easiest way possible for a green horse—with his movement balanced— use a long enough diagonal to give him plenty of time to straighten before you ask him to bend the other way (A to D). Then move your horse on an angle to his line of travel while you confirm that he is moving well into the outside hand (D to E). Finally, you can just follow his bend into the new direction (E to F).

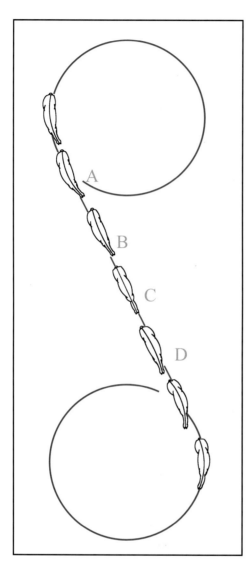

A

B

C

D

Figure 61 To teach your horse to go with an even bend and with no angle to his line, come off the circle at point A. Release the bend at B, allow him to straighten at C, and pick up the new bend at D. The difference between this and figure 60 is that rather than continuing to encourage more bend and angle as you have been doing, use your outside hand and leg to gently say, "Thank you, that's quite enough."

When a horse is perfectly willing to over bend and move away from your inside leg, while allowing your outside rein to prevent him from bending too much, and your outside leg to stop him from drifting off his line of travel, you have achieved the ideal—an evenly bent horse, ridden forward from inside leg to outside hand and leg. The mystery is solved. Here is the theory and practice.

In order for your horse to bend evenly and carry you with no angle to his line of travel, he must be strong enough to raise his back, engage his hind legs, and balance his weight from front to back. How do you know if he's ready? Try it. If he accepts the exercise and you feel like he becomes turbocharged when he's straight, then he's ready. If it's a lot of work for him, back off for a few weeks and keep building topline muscle.

The process of bending your horse evenly and keeping him from drifting out is simplicity itself. Put him on a figure of eight with nice long diagonals and change bend and direction just as you have been doing with the same over bend and drift that your horse is used to. Start across the diagonal, release the bend, move him into the new outside hand then ask him for more bend and angle. Now on each change of direction simply allow less bend than you did before. After a few times back and forth your horse will have an even bend and stay on his line of travel.

It's also very common to feel as if there's a train behind you pushing your horse along. This is the energy of your horse's hind legs coming through his back.

The aids for this are exactly the same as you've been using. First soften your outside hand to release the bend and bump him lightly with your outside leg.

As the horse begins to straighten, brush him lightly with your new outside leg as if to say, "Thanks, that's what I wanted," and establish contact with the new outside hand. Well, I told you it was simple. It's so simple it's hard to write about—there's nothing new, or more for you to do. It's all about you doing less.

When your horse is evenly bent and on his line, his withers will be right in front of your belly button. You'll probably feel as though they have lifted vertically as well. This is a result of your horse accepting more weight on his hind legs and adjusting his weight balance from front to rear.

It's also very common to feel as if there's a train behind you pushing your horse along. This is the energy of your horse's hind legs coming through his back. All the muscle you've been putting on with all that lateral work is now directed straight ahead. It's cool—you'll like it!

Most horses react to the feeling of carrying a rider correctly as they react to sweet feed. They like it! It's not at all unusual for them to offer a little medium or even extended trot on their own.

All of this is good, very good, but you have to be the responsible adult. Remember Rule Number 2, *Reward in Proportion*, and that he's using fairly new muscles in a slightly different way. They will likely tire easily and you need to keep him enjoying the feeling of carrying you the right way. So, the

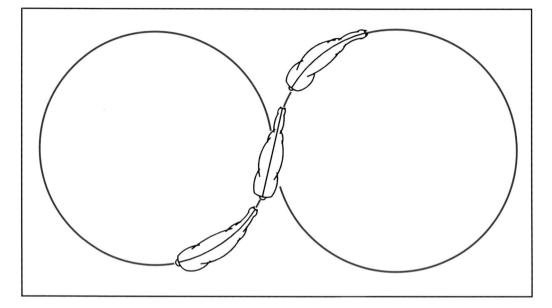

Figure 62 An advanced horse can do a correct change of bend and direction in just three strides. When ridden this well, it feels as though you've tossed the horse from one outside rein to the other as easily as you might toss a ball from one hand to the other.

first day, do a few steps and immediately reward with an allowed stop. Maybe you can do two or three diagonals like that, and then call it a day. Get off while he still wants to do more.

The next day, begin as you have been doing—allowing your horse as much bend and angle as he is comfortable with. Toward the end of your ride, do another two or three diagonals with an even bend. And on the following day do the same, but allow him to take a few more of those nice big through steps. Keep increasing the number of steps on the diagonal until you run out of it and begin to go around the half circle at the end of it. As days go by he'll learn to keep the bend even while doing the entire figure eight and then eventually just to always keep his bend even.

When that happens, it's time to introduce canter work, real transitions and half-halts. As you progress with them, you'll find that you need less and less time on the diagonal to change your horse's bend and direction. Eventually, you'll be able to do an advanced change of bend and direction in just three strides, as shown in figure 62.

22

Half-Halts

A horse half-halts by stepping further under his body with his hind legs and accepting more weight on them. This increased engagement collects the horse and makes it easier for him to change his gait or direction. This explanation of what a half-halts is and why you ask a horse to do one is straight-forward and well known, yet use of the half-halt continues to confuse many and be surrounded by misconception.

Often, a lot of the confusion begins when the half-halt is taught as an aid the rider gives instead of an exercise the horse does. This leads to the misconception that every horse, at any stage of training, can half-halt if the rider just asks correctly.

Many riders are taught—or believe—they can give a half-halt by pulling on, or doing what is often called "squeezing the reins." There is even a commonly heard analogy about asking for a half-halt by squeezing the rein as though squeezing water out of a sponge. Well, squeezing the rein can eventually teach the

Often, a lot of the confusion begins when the half-halt is taught as an aid the rider gives instead of an exercise the horse does.

horse that it means, "I-would-very-much-appreciate-it-if-you-would-slow-down-just-a-very-small-amount-thank-you-very-much." As horses are the wonderful, intelligent, courteous creatures they are, they sometimes take pity on our feeble efforts at communication and may slow down when we squeeze the daylights out of that poor imaginary sponge. But that's a slow down - not a half-halt.

Before you can ask a horse to half-halt he must be strong enough to raise his back and engage his hind legs.

In a *slow down*, the horse's tempo becomes slower, his energy output is diminished, and his stride becomes shorter and choppier. In a *half-halt*, the horse's tempo and energy output remain constant while his stride becomes higher and rounder as he collects. When you consider these differences it becomes perfectly obvious that before you can ask a horse to half-halt he must be strong enough to raise his back and engage his hind legs.

You'll know your horse is ready when he can sustain working gaits with an equal bend from poll to dock, change his bend and direction with a constant tempo and length of stride while always swinging his back and maintaining a soft, quiet contact. His muscles should be developed enough so that it is easy for him to hold his head and neck out with the poll a few inches above the level of the withers.

Since physical development alone is not enough, you will also need a way to teach your horse about the half-halt and toward this end that I offer a series of exercises for you to do with him. The progression of exercises is as follows: the *allowed stop* (with which your horse should be well acquainted by now), the *soft stop*, *stepping up*, and finally, *halts* and *half-halts*, which are each used to assist in the development of each other.

The Soft Stop

Up to this point in this book, I have only discussed asking your horse to stop by using the *allowed stop* and, in a pinch, the *just-plain-stop rein*. When the allowed stop is used you release the reins and a give a pat on the neck. This should be confirmed enough by now so that when your horse feels you beginning to give the reins he begins to stop. The first step to building a half-halt is an exercise I call the *soft stop*. The soft stop is a combination of the allowed stop and the mounted softening exercises that the horse has been performing.

The procedure is incredibly simple. First, begin the allowed stop by sitting up straighter and softening the reins as though about to release them, but do not completely drop them. As the horse stops, proceed immediately to ask him to soften. It should only take a few minutes for the horse to understand that he should first stop, and then immediately soften, as both exercises are familiar to him by now. Once he does this, begin to blur the line between the two exercises. Ask the horse to soften as he is beginning to stop but still moving. Again, as these exercises are familiar, it should take very little time to make the request clear.

It is important that the horse be allowed to reach forward with his head and neck a little during this stage. No attempt should be made to keep the horse together; rather, he should be asked to stay soft and be allowed to reach out as he does so. In other words, you must still allow the horse to stretch his back and neck in the downward transition so that he finds it easy to bring his hind legs forward. It amazes new riders that the horse will always complete the stop as the reins are released, not as they are applied. This reaction to the release of the reins is a testimonial to the necessity of allowing the horse the freedom to bring his legs up under him. On a "made" horse, this reaction is much less obvious, as the horse has already learned to soften within his body and give himself the freedom to engage without visibly stretching over the topline.

Stepping Up

After the horse has come to the point of consistently offering a soft stop, you may ask for each hind leg in its turn to step up a little. I find it's best to introduce this concept by doing a little in-hand work with him at the end of the day's ride.

Asking the horse to step up from the ground is almost the same as asking the horse to step away from the whip you did in exercises in Chapter 18, *Soften, Bend, Move into the Hand*. The difference is that before you were working in the middle of the ring so your horse could take a lateral step away from you when you touched him with the whip, and you allowed him to bend as much as he wanted. For this stepping-up exercise, you will work against the wall, so the horse cannot step away (fig. 63). Just as in the earlier exercise, bridge both reins in one hand and tap him gently near the hock with the whip.

As with all new exercises your horse will go through a trial-and-error period while he figures out what it is you want. Typically, when introducing stepping up, he will try to walk straight through your hand. When he does, you need to give and take on the reins and stop him.

It's not at all unusual for a horse to try and back up once he realizes he's not allowed to go forward. When he does, just walk back with him, continu-

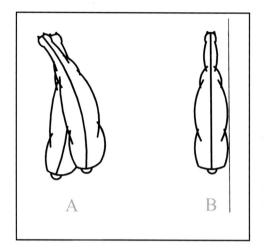

Figure 63 *When you asked the horse to step laterally away from you in earlier groundwork, you were in the middle of the ring, so he had room to step away (A). To ask the horse to step up, work along the wall instead, so he has to move his legs forward instead of over (B).*

ing to gently tap him near the hock. Eventually he'll get tired of backing up and try something else, or he'll back himself into a corner and that will stop him. Either is fine. When he stops backing up, give him a pat and gently lead him to where you began, and then start again.

Frequently, a horse will kick out at the whip. Just as you did in the earlier softening exercise, don't react to it. Simply keep touching him until he realizes that kicking out isn't useful and he tries something else.

Eventually, he'll simply pick his foot up and put it down again. When he does, reward him. That is all that's required of this exercise—when you touch his rear leg with the whip, he should just pick his foot up and put it down. It's nice if he brings it a little forward and puts it down; eventually he will, but for now if he just stays completely relaxed, picks his foot up, and puts it down in the same spot, you have succeeded.

Once he has the idea of just picking his rear foot up when you ask, modify the exercise as follows: walk along the wall, come to a stop, ask him to pick up his foot, and then walk off again. It should only take a few minutes at the end of each day's work for a week or so, for him to be able to do this in both directions while staying completely relaxed. Then, ask for the same thing from the saddle.

Just walk along the wall, ask your horse to stop and soften, and then pick one hind foot up and put it down. If the horse has stopped squarely, begin with either foot; otherwise, with a light bump of your leg, or by tapping him lightly with the whip, ask the horse to move whichever leg is furthest to the rear a little forward. Once he has moved one hind leg forward, ask him to move the next. At first it makes no difference how long it takes to move each foot forward. What is important is that the horse softens throughout his body as he moves his hind foot forward.

You'll know he's soft if the reins stay soft and he picks up the hind leg in question and moves it but nothing else. If he stiffens against your hands and tries to stick his nose out and run through your hand when you ask for this, it's probably best to get off and repeat the groundwork until he understands it better.

Half-Halt in the Walk

As the horse gets the idea that every time he comes to a soft stop he is going to be asked to step up a little with the hind legs, he begins to anticipate this movement. Good! In a little time, the actions of soft stop, followed by step up, step up, run into each another. Just ask the horse to stop, but before he stops *completely*, ask for one hind leg to step up, then the other, and finally, ask him to continue to walk. So, from the walk, it becomes: *almost* a soft stop; step up; step up; walk on. In other words, it's a half-halt.

As this sequence is smoothed out, the aids are too. By the time your horse is doing a half-halt, you need only sit up a bit straighter and apply a light leg. If you bother with the reins at all, it should not amount to anything more than a slight vibration.

Trying to create elevation or engagement mechanically is unnecessary because you have properly prepared him for the movement physically and then presented it to him in a way that made it easy for him to understand.

When the horse realizes that he will be asked to walk on after he has stepped up, he will also realize that he is only being asked to perform "half of a halt," not a complete stop. Then he will discover that the easiest way to manage this task is by softening and elevating his front end and back as he does so. Note that the horse is elevating himself and beginning to collect on his own. There is no need to try and lift his forehand, push his back end, or drive him up to the bit. In fact, any attempt to do so will be counterproductive.

Trying to create elevation or engagement mechanically is unnecessary because you have properly prepared him for the movement physically and then presented it to him in a way that made it easy for him to understand. Your job now is to avoid interfering with him doing his job. Yes, it really is this easy if you forget about squeezing that silly sponge and just explain to your horse how to do "half-of-a-halt".

Half-Halt in the Trot

Half-halts in the trot begin with trot, walk, step up, step up, trot on. The horse soon figures out the pattern and is more than willing to eliminate the intermediate walk transitions as he progresses. Soon you can do trot; *almost* walk; step up; trot. At this stage of training the aids should be invisible from the ground and almost imperceptible to you—more of a thought than an action. It's just a slight upward motion of your chest and light touch of leg.

Half-Halt in the Canter

You may recall from Chapter 20, *Falling In and Out* that I said that the canter, having a lot of momentum and speed, is not a suitable gait for teaching a horse how to deal with balance issues. But, now that your horse has gained strength from work on his Natural Circle, learned to carry you with an even bend by changing his bend and direction correctly, and has been introduced to half-halts in the walk and trot, it's time to begin "work" in the canter.

I wait until this stage of training to introduce "work" in the canter because until horses have these preliminary skills, there just isn't very much that can be done in this gait. In fact, I'm certain that most of the so-called behavioral problems that come to me have their roots in asking too much too soon in the canter. This is especially true with tall horses as they have more difficulty learning to balance riders to begin with. So if the canter is forced on them before they can deal with it comfortably, they start to fear being cantered and then they begin to dislike being ridden altogether. Note that it's perfectly fine to allow your horse to canter at an earlier stage (especially out on the trail) but now you can begin to ask for correct work in the schooling ring, on circles, and curves that require a degree of engagement.

The canter stride has three beats and a moment of suspension. The order in which the hooves hit the ground is: outside hind; inside hind and outside fore together; then the inside fore followed by the moment of suspension during which all four feet are in the air. It is during the moment of suspension that the horse makes changes in his weight, balance, and stride, so the aids for the next stride of the canter have to be given before the moment of suspension in the current one.

For example, if you want to do a flying change from the right lead to the left, you have to give the aids for the change to the left lead before the moment of suspension of the current stride. Then, while all of the horse's feet are in the air he can switch things around and land on his new outside hind. The same is true when asking for a half-halt. Since you want the horse to bring his hind legs under him and he has to do it while they are in the air, you must make the request just before the moment of suspension. Then you can "encourage and allow" him during the moment of suspension by releasing your aids so that he is free to bring his hind legs forward.

Teaching the horse to engage in the canter should not be difficult after he has learned to anticipate bringing his legs up in the walk and trot transitions. By working from canter to walk and back to canter, the horse will begin to engage so that he's ready to perform as requested. With a little time, you can ask for the transition to walk and then, as the horse collects in preparation for the downward transition, encourage and allow him to continue in the canter. This is a canter half-halt and if you ask for one every stride you will be riding a collected canter.

The Halt

Once the horse has the idea of a correct half-halt, proceeding to a halt is child's play. After one good "half-of-a-halt," immediately ask for the second "half-of-the-halt," and it is a complete halt.

A correctly performed halt requires no more collection than was asked for by the first half-halt. Since the horse has already swung his legs forward under himself and brought his back up in response to the first half-halt, you keep your legs on as the halt is completed. It feels as though your legs are holding the horse's hind legs forward, which keeps his back up and creates the halt.

It's quite wonderful to canter along, and then, in a moment of suspension, ask for a half-halt and simply hold the horse's legs forward and his back up for a tiny bit longer with a light touch of your own legs on him. The horse should come straight down into a perfectly square halt in less time than it takes for the second half of a canter stride. There should not be any "sliding" stop, and the contact should remain absolutely the same or perhaps even the tiniest bit softer. The horse simply picks himself up as though he is going to take another collected stride and puts himself down in the halt. It should appear as though the horse has landed in feathers—soft, smooth, and easy. To make it more interesting, the difference between coming down in the halt, or in extended canter, is in terms of the aids, a razor's edge. It's more a question of timing and inflection, than of different aids.

The difference between a halt and a stop is not just a fine point. In terms of what is going on within the horse, they are opposites. The halt sustains energy; the stop dissipates it.

A halt like this is simply not possible with a horse that does not understand how to collect and have the ability to do so. To create a *stop* with a greener horse, the energy has to be allowed to dissipate over several strides—the momentum gradually reduced until the forward inertia is overcome. When stopping a green horse, the possibility of deciding at the last moment to extend the gait instead of halting does not exist. If it were attempted, it would take at least several strides for the horse to start firing up the boiler again, shift his weight, and gradually begin to lengthen his strides.

The difference between a halt and a stop is not just a fine point. In terms of what is going on within the horse, they are opposites. The halt sustains energy; the stop dissipates it. It's an important difference because if it is not said differently, thought of differently, trained differently, and ridden differently, the halt degenerates into a quick stop when the rider slams on the brakes. He yanks on the horse's mouth and grinds down with his seat—both actions that actually prevent the horse from engaging and performing the correct halt.

Half-halts and halts are wonderful, glorious little exercises. Take the time to do them perfectly. Don't cheat yourself and partner by confusing them with slow downs and stops.

23
Transitions

Excellent transitions are attainable by every rider on every horse. Later in training, compromises will have to be made for a horse's conformation and overall talent. However, as you polish your horse's basic training, perfection can and should be achieved no matter what deficiencies are present.

Before your horse became proficient at stepping up, and doing half-halts, your only concern when making a transition was to keep the movement balanced. So you changed gaits by moving your horse at an angle to his line as you sent him out to the walk or trot, on his Natural Circle (fig. 64A). However, just as a slow down isn't a half-halt, and a stop isn't a halt, that wasn't really doing a transition. That was going from one gait to another in a way that helped the horse stay balanced.

When doing proper transitions from one gait to another, your horse maintains an even bend, remains exactly on his line of travel, and keeps his even tempo (fig. 64B).

Upward Transitions

Your horse will have to be proficient at stepping up in order to do a proper transition because it begins in the hind legs.

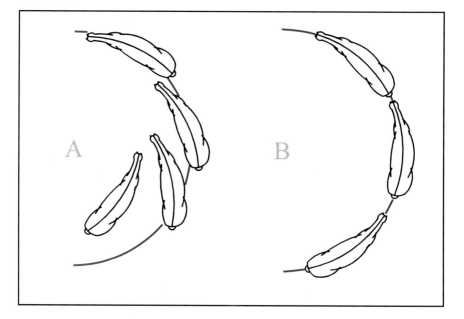

Figure 64 *When your primary concern was teaching your horse to maintain his balance, you went from gait to gait by moving your horse out to the circle and keeping him at an angle to his line (A). To do a real transition, keep your horse evenly bent and on his line of travel as you ask for the new gait (B).*

For example, when a horse at a halt is asked to walk off, he should soften in the jaw, poll, and neck as he steps up with at least one hind leg. In other words, the horse softens into the transition. He moves up to the hand and engages before he moves his body.

Conversely, if the horse stiffens against the hand and throws his head out before stepping off, he has stiffened into the transition. This is worthless. Before the first step is taken the horse is already against the aids, stiff, and hollow-backed. Now the rider is faced with correcting the walk before the first step has been completed! Rather than deal with this situation, it is always better to stop the horse (use the *just-plain-stop* rein aid—a correct halt is impossible in these circumstances), soften him again, and then try for a proper transition to the walk, or whatever gait is desired. As a practical matter, if the horse is showing an inclination to walk through the hand in transitions, it may be better to have him a little too soft for a while, even a hair behind the vertical, with a small amount of slack in the reins. This is not ideal, but it avoids misunderstanding and seesawing the reins through the transition.

By and large, all that the rider ever needs to keep in mind during upward transitions is that the horse has to stay balanced and soft. This is really all the rider should concern himself with. So what to do if the horse stiffens? Follow the rules: temporarily abandon the immediate goal of walking, trotting, or cantering and make the goal a good transition. Is that simple? Yes. Is it simplistic? No. When the emphasis is placed on keeping the horse balanced and soft rather than making him go, the result is a horse that learns to stay balanced and goes softly. It may take several minutes to make that point. So what?

Halt to Walk

The actual procedure to ask for a walk with the horse softened in the halt is to sit up a bit, press your belly button out, tickle with your calf, and allow the horse to step into a following hand. If your horse pulls on the rein and tries to stick his nose out as he steps off, stop him and repeat the procedure.

If you don't get a good halt-to-walk transition after just a few tries, get off and work from the ground. The horse is saying he hasn't been prepared well enough with stepping up, has forgotten, or is confused. Review the in-hand work in Chapter 22, and then remount and try again.

When the emphasis is placed on keeping the horse balanced and soft rather than making him go, the result is a horse that learns to stay balanced and goes softly.

Trot Transition

Once the horse has shown consistent transitions to the walk, correct work with trot transitions can begin. The aids for the trot transition are the same as for the walk, only slightly more prolonged. During the halt-to-trot transition a few steps of walk are not a problem as long as the horse stays soft going from halt to walk, and walk to trot. In time he will learn to differentiate between transitions to the walk and trot, and eliminate the walk steps in between.

Canter Transitions

The canter transition often presents a problem to green horses and riders. A rider in the walk or trot asks the horse for a canter and the horse picks up the running trot and then falls into the canter. A terrible thing to do! One thousand pounds of mass, tripping about, barely able to stay upright. This is simply not an acceptable training technique. Rather than teaching the horse to canter, it teaches the horse to be afraid to canter.

Teaching the horse the canter transition from the walk instead of the trot discourages the horse from running into the canter. For this reason, I usually teach the walk-to-canter transition first. After the horse is fairly well confirmed in the canter itself, trot to canter and canter to trot come easily and naturally.

The correct aids for the canter consist of the rider sitting up straighter, moving his outside leg back a bit, and having the horse move slightly more into the outside aids. It feels more as though the horse is being *moved* into the outside leg, rather than the outside leg being moved into the horse. A fine point, but that is the way it feels when done correctly. Although many texts suggest the rider adjust his seat and weight·during the transition, I've found that merely moving the outside leg back is sufficient. Deliberate attempts by the rider to weight his seat, more often result in an exaggerated contortion than in a proper aid.

When asked for a canter from the walk, the horse has two choices as far as you are concerned. He can walk a few steps more and then canter, or he can canter immediately. If he breaks into the trot, ask him to stop and then repeat the request. The horse will go through the process of trying to figure out what is being asked. He may try backing up. "No, that isn't it." Or he may try a leg-yield of sorts. "Sorry, that's not it either. Try again." Eventually he will try to canter. There are, after all, only so many possibilities.

If there is a question, "Does the horse understand that I'm asking for the canter?" then a few compromises may be allowed regarding the quality of the gait and transition. You may have to accept some falling in or out or a bit of unevenness at the beginning. These compromises may be necessary until you believe the horse understands that these aids mean canter. Once you're confident he understands, begin asking for better and better quality transitions.

One of the "tricks" I use with a horse that has been poorly schooled in the past (as opposed to a green horse) is to allow him to counter-bend slightly at first. Generally, he has been asked to canter with his neck bent to the outside and thrown on to his inside shoulder with a strong outside leg as the "cue." If the horse will canter in response to these signals, I use them, and as soon as possible begin to decrease the amount of bend until the horse is straight (no bend in this context), then continue the reversal until the horse is beginning to bend correctly into the transition. The whole process of retraining canter transitions should take about ten to fifteen minutes the first day. It will no doubt have to be repeated for several days until the horse fully understands how to perform a canter transition correctly.

You should be able to develop a very credible collected canter in your horse just by schooling the walk-to-canter transition, followed by a few steps of canter, and then a transition to walk again. Since your horse will have to engage to make a proper transition from walk to canter, and then again to make the transition from canter to walk, he will soon begin to anticipate and remain engaged, ready to perform the downward transition for those few strides. In short, he will be doing a collected canter.

You'll recognize that your horse has collected his canter when everything gets softer, and you have the sensation of being drawn "into" the saddle so your seat feels "stuck" to it. It may seem as though your horse's feet are barely touching the ground, and if you listen carefully even the sound of his hoof beats will be quieter.

On every step of the collected canter, you need to ask your horse to stay engaged with requests for a half-halt, and then, within the same stride, a request to continue cantering. However, these requests must be made with aids so slight they are invisible to anyone watching. Riding this well, you may wonder if you are asking your horse to continue each stride, or if he is asking permission from you for each and every step he takes. Once you experience this feeling, you'll begin to understand how it is possible for a fully trained horse to perform extensions, flying changes, and pirouettes.

You'll recognize that your horse has collected his canter when everything gets softer, and you have the sensation of being drawn "into" the saddle so your seat feels "stuck" to it.

Downward Transitions

Downward transitions from one gait to another are just that, a change of gait only. When you change gait, only the rhythm should change. Your horse should keep the same energy and tempo.

The basic procedure for a downward transition is to first do a half-halt so your horse is engaged and ready then *break* the rhythm. I explained about the need to use your aids in time with the horse's rhythm in Chapter 6, *The Aids of Reason*. Well, I hope you've been doing this because in order to break the rhythm, you need to use your aids out of rhythm for a moment. The better you've been working in your horse's rhythm, the more subtle your aids for the transition will be and the less his tempo, stride, and energy will be affected by them.

Interestingly, it doesn't make much difference which aid or aids you use out of rhythm. Certainly it's worth trying to "not follow" with your seat for a moment. A touch of the rein at just the "wrong" moment will certainly encourage any horse to break gait. In the previous chapter you saw how legs could be used to finish a halt, so there are definite possibilities with them too.

Yes, there are some very detailed descriptions around that explain exactly which muscles to use, and in what order, but a transition should take place in a single stride, half of which you've already used for a half-halt. There is not much time left to think about your various muscle groups when you need to finish the transition while maintaining the energy and tempo.

I suppose I could try and tell you exactly how I use my aids out of rhythm for each transition, but I'm not entirely sure I know myself and I'm pretty certain they wouldn't work as well for you anyway. After all, what are the chances that you and I will ever ride exactly alike?

The simple fact is, by the time you're going for the perfect transition, you're beginning to ride in a way that is and will be very personal to you. Your height, weight, and personality will now make you the unique rider that you will become. So, I will tell you again, in a correct downward transition, only the rhythm changes —the energy and tempo remain. Ask for a half-halt then break the rhythm.

24 Conclusion

If the ending of the last chapter left you feeling a bit unsatisfied, or abandoned, I have to admit it was a bit contrived. I wanted to make the point that you have the tools you need to move on. I'm not suggesting that you never need to take another lesson, and this isn't the last book on riding and training you'll ever need to read either, but I hope you'll get a little more out of your future lessons and reading because of this book. And yes, you'll need more training tips and techniques too, but you'll be able to sort out the ones that help from the ones that hurt you and your horse.

Although this book is about teaching a horse to carry a rider correctly, it's impossible to gain a better understanding of basics without becoming a better rider. It makes no difference whether you know about balancing a horse's motion in terms of my technical explanation, or, if you "know" it from the feel of walking on your own Natural Circle. You'll never again confuse a horse out of balance with a horse resisting, and settle for throwing on a tighter noseband or more severe bit. And it will never occur to you that the feeling of your horse wrapping himself around you and moving so loosely that he seems to melt away as you show him his Natural Circle from the ground, could be duplicated by poking him with a spur or hitting him with a whip.

If I've made my case, you've made a trade. In exchange for a few silly words like *resistance* and *evasion*, words that never did any rider any good at all, you have rules and a philosophy that work. Instead of a tack box full of bits and pieces of leather and metal all finely finished, all made of the highest quality materials, and all designed to cover up problems, you have a straightforward method of solving problems. You've made a good deal.

...movements are really nothing more than demonstrations of good basics.

But don't underestimate how much practical training has been covered and just how far along in your training program it will take you. For instance, if your horse knows how to lengthen, collect, and turn correctly, just point him to the next fence and, for the most part, stay out of his way. If you need to set him up or adjust his stride, you can do it with subtle little movements, a slight give and take with the reins or perhaps brace your back for a moment. That's all that is required to jump a horse that has learned to keep his own balance and you only use the reins for guidance.

Dressage movements are really nothing more than demonstrations of good basics. The shoulder-in is just moving at an angle to the line of travel with an even bend from poll to dock. Using aids in rhythm, you can build a half-pass by asking your horse for bend on one stride and to move over on the next. A flying change is simply a transition from canter to canter, and the piaffe and passage are just gaits that develop when a horse half-halts very, very well. With good basics, all of dressage can be explained in a paragraph. Without them, the hundreds of volumes describing individual movements and specific training techniques are not enough. Indeed, if dressage be the goal, this is the stuff it's made of.

It always comes down to basics. If things are going well, it's because your horse's basics are good. If things aren't going so well, invariably there's a problem with them. It makes no difference if you're starting a brand new baby or trying to improve your mount of many years, it always comes down to the quality of your horse's working gaits, half-halts, and transitions.

Glossary

Please note this list is intended to describe these movements, not define them.

Flying Change: The horse changes his canter lead during the moment of suspension. For example, he leaves the ground on his left lead and lands cantering on his right lead. Flying changes can be performed in a series, typically every fourth, third, second, or single stride.

Half-pass: A lateral movement in which the horse moves diagonally, and bent in the direction he is traveling toward. For example, he is bent to the left and moves forward and sideways to the left.

Passage: A very collected trot in which the movement is high and round with a clear moment of hesitation.

Piaffe: An extremely collected movement in which the horse trots in place, or very nearly in place.

Pirouette: A movement in which the evenly bent horse pivots around his inside hind leg into the direction of his bend while maintaining his tempo and rhythm.

Shoulder-in: A lateral movement performed on a straight line or circle on three tracks. The horse is evenly bent in one direction, but moves forward away from the bend. For example, the horse is bent to the left, but moves forward and to the right. It's common to ride a horse on a circle, or along the side of the schooling ring in shoulder-in.

Turn on the Forehand: A movement in which the horse pivots around the inside foreleg. Western trainers often say the back end goes around the front end to describe this type of movement.

Index

Page numbers in *italics* indicate illustrations

Aids, 43–85
  against the aids, 26
  allowing, 44–45, 46, 47
  behind the aids, 27
  changing, 43–44
  consistency of, 45–46
  conversations, 44–45
  corrections vs., 43, 49
  encouraging, 44–47
  exercise-reward, 43, 49–50
  force of, 44, 50–51
  meaning of, 45–47
  mechanical effect, 45
  releasing, 44–45, 46, 47, 82
  requests, 44–45, 46
  rhythm, 40, 44, 195–196
  running through, 26–27
  silence, 44–45, 46, 47
  softening to, 26–28
  whip, 118, 127, 130, 154
  See also Balance; Contact; Rein aids; Seat
Allowed stop, 23–24, 126, 132, *137*, 139
Allowing aids, 44–45, 46, 47
Angle, 38, *38*, 99

Balance, 89–111
  angle, 38, *38*, 99
  bend, 38, *38*, 99, 100, 102–111, *104, 110*
  direction and, 37, 99
  energy, 37, *95*, 95–97, *97*
  on the forehand, 89–92, *90*
  lateral movements, 100
  Natural Circle, 102–111, *104, 110*
  natural tempo, 94, *94*, 95
  rein aids and, 83–84
  reward in proportion, 108–109
  saddle work, 169–170
  speed/tempo/stride, 40, 93–97, *94–95, 97*
  straight line, 157, *157*
  topline and, 40, *41*, *90*, 91
  true balance, 93–97, *94–95, 97*
  weight, 175–182, *177, 179–180, 182*
  working gaits, 89–92, *90*
  See also Ground work; Saddle work;
  Work in hand
Becker, Nicole Uphoff, 96
Behind the aids, 27
Bend, 38, *39*
  balance, 99, 100, 102–111, *104, 110*
  changing, 175–182, *177, 179–180, 182*
  under saddle, 162, *163*
Bits, 118, 130
Bracing back (rider's), 58
Bridles, 118, 130

Cantering, 188–189, 193–195, 199
Circles. *See* Longeing; Natural Circle
Collection, 40, *41*
Comfort vs. pain, 20–21

Contact, 61–71
  elbows (rider's), 64, 67, *68*
  shoulders (rider's), 64–67, *65–66*
  See also Aids; Rein aids; Seat
Conversation (aids), 44–45
Corrections, 28–29, 43, 49–51

Desensitization, 127–128
Direction
  balance and, 37, 99
  changing, 175–182, *177, 179–180, 182*
Direct rein, 74

Elasticity, 36–37
Elbows (rider's), 64, 67, *68*
Elevation, 40, *41*
Encouraging (aids), 44–47
Energy
  balance and, 37, *95*, 95–97, *97*
  excess, 118–120, *119*, 152
Engagement, 40, *41*
Evasion, 4, 12, 26, 198
Every step counts, 26–28
Exercise-reward cycle
  aids, 43, 49–50
  ground exercises, 116
  training, 7–9, 11–12
  work in hand, 130, 151–152

Falling in/out, 145, 169–174, *171, 173*
Flexions, 131–132, *133–136*
Flying changes, 199
Frame, 40

Gaits, 40
  canter, 188–189, 193–195, 199
  trot, 168, 188, 193
  walk, 187
  working, 89–92, *90*
Giving reins, 67, *69*, 84
Ground work, 115–128
  desensitization, 127–128
  energy, excess, 118–120, *119*, 152
  exercise-reward, 116
  ground tying, 123–126, *126*
  herding, 115–116
  latching on, 116–117, *117*
  leading, 120–122, *121*
  tack for, 118
  turning, 122–123, *123–125*
  whip aid, 118, 127
  See also Longeing; Work in hand
"Guessing" (horse's), 12

Half-halts, 91–92, 183–190, *186*
Half-pass, 199
Half release, 74, *75*
Halts, 189–190, 193
Hands, 42. *See also* Rein aids

Head position (rider's), 59
Herding, 115–116
Hitchhiker rein, 74–78, *76–77*

Indirect rein, 80, 85
In-hand exercises. *See* Work in hand
Inside, 41–42, 131

Just-plain-stop, 78–80, *79*

Konyot, Alex, 53

Latching on, 116–117, *117*
Lateral movements, 100
Lead changes, 199
Leading, 120–122, *121*
Leaning on reins, 82, 83
Learning to learn, 11–15
Lengthening stride, *158*, 159
Lightness, 36
Longeing, 150–159
    circle size, 154, *155–156*
    holding longe, 153–154
    lengthening stride, *158*, 159
    shoulder-in, *158*, 159, 199
    side reins, 152–153, *153*
    stopping, 118–119, *119*
    straight line, 157, *157*
    whip aid, 154
    See also Work in hand
Love-of-the-game, 24–26

Memory (horse's), 12–13
Mouth (horse's), 84, 85
Muscle knots (horse's), 139, *141*, 141–142, *143*
Mutually Assured Destruction (M.A.D.), 19

Natural Circle
    balance, 102–111, *104*, *110*
    saddle work, 164, *166–167*, 166–168
    work in hand, 147–150, *149*, *151*
Natural tempo, 94, *94*, 95
No one gets hurt, 19–21
Noseband (cavesson), 130

On the forehand, 89–92, *90*
Opening rein, 74
Outmaneuvering, 19–20
Outside, 41, 42, 131
Over bending, 139, *140*

Pain vs. comfort, 20–21
Passage, 199
Patience, 30–31
Piaffe, 199
Pirouette, 199
Play, 14–15, *15*, 19, 20
Position, 53–54, *55*. *See also* Contact; Seat
Pulling, 36, 83

Quarters, moving
    saddle work, 162, 164, *165*
    work in hand, 145–147, *146*, *148*

Rein aids, 73–85
    adjusting, *70*, 70–71
    advanced horses, 81, 82
    balance and, 83–84
    direct rein, 74
    giving, 67, *69*, 84
    green horses, 73–80, 81, 82
    half release, 74, *75*
    hitchhiker, 74–78, *76–77*
    holding reins, *63*, 63–64, *144*, 145
    indirect rein, 80, 85
    just-plain-stop, 78–80, *79*
    leaning on, 82, 83
    mouth (horse's), 84, 85
    opening rein, 74
    pulling on, 36, 83
    releasing the rein, 82
    seat and, 67, 70
    stretching, 36, 83
    See also Contact; Saddle work; Work in hand
Relaxation, 37, 131
Releasing aids, 44–45, 46, 47, 82
Reliability/trustworthiness, 24
Rembrandt, 96
Repetitions, 29
Requests (aids), 44–45, 46
Resistance, 4, 12, 14, 26, 198
Reward in proportion, 21–26, 108–109, 174, 181–182
Rhythm, 40, 44, 195–196
Riding terms, 35–42
Rules (training), 17–31
    allowed stop, 23–24
    approach to, 30–31
    big picture and, 30
    correction, not punishment, 28–29
    every step counts, 26–28
    interpretation of, 18
    love-of-the-game, 24–26
    no one gets hurt, 19–21
    outmaneuvering horses, 19–20
    pain vs. comfort, 20–21
    patience, 30–31
    reliability/trustworthiness, 24
    repetitions, 29
    reward in proportion, 21–26, 108–109, 174, 181–182
    simplifying vs. qualifying, 28–29
    softening to aids, 26–28
    taking your time, 29–31
    See also Training basics
Running through aids, 26–27

Saddles, 54, 56, *56*
Saddle work, 161–196

assistant for, 161–162
balance and, 169–170, 175–182, *177, 179–180, 182*
bend/direction, changing, 175–182, *177, 179–180, 182*
bending, 162, *163*
cantering, 188–189, 193–195, 199
falling in/out, 169–174, *171, 173*
half-halts, 91–92, 183–190, *186*
halts, 189–190, 193
Natural Circle, 164, *166–167*, 166–168
reward in proportion, 174, 181–182
rhythm, 40, 195–196
shoulders/quarters, 162, 164, *165*
softening, 162
soft stop, 184–185
"squeezing the reins," 183–184
stepping up, 185–187, *186*
stops vs. halts, 190
transitions, 191–196, *192*
trotting, 168, 188, 193
walk, 187
See also Aids; Balance; Work in hand
Seat (independent), 53–59
bracing your back, 58
head position, 59
legs and, 56–57
lightening, 58
position for, 53–54, *55*
rein aids and, 67, 70
saddles and, 54, 56, *56*
straightness, 57, *57–59*
See also Contact
Secretariat, 96
Shoulder-in, *158*, 159, 199
Shoulders (rider's), 64–67, *65–66*
Shoulders, moving
saddle work, 162, 164, *165*
work in hand, 145–147, *146, 148*
Side reins, 152–153, *153*
Silence (aids), 44–45, 46, 47
Simplifying vs. qualifying, 28–29
Slow downs, 184
Snaffle bits, 118, 130
Snaffle rein, *63*, 63–64
Softening, 36
to aids, 26–28
body (horse's), 142, *144*, 144–145
jaw/poll, 131–132, *133–136*
under saddle, 162
Soft hands, 42
Soft stop, 184–185
Speed/tempo/stride, 40, 93–97, *94–95, 97*
"Squeezing the reins," 183–184
Staying soft, *138*, 139
Stepping up, 185–187, *186*
Stiff/still hands, 42

Stopping
allowed stop, 23–24, 126, 132, *137*, 139
halts vs., 190
just-plain-stop, 78–80, *79*
longeing, 118–119, *119*
soft stop, 184–185
Straightness (seat), 57, *57–59*
Stretching, 36, 83
Stride, 40, 93–97, *94–95, 97*

Tack, 118, 130
Taking your time, 29–31
Tempo, 40, 44, 93–97, *94–95, 97*
Topline, 40, *41, 90*, 91
Training basics, 3–32
corrections, 28–29, 43, 49–51
exercise-reward, 7–9, 11–12
"guessing" (horse's), 12
importance of, 3–5, 197–198
learning, 11–15
memory of horse, 12–13
partnership, 3–5
play, 14–15, *15*, 19, 20
resistance, 4, 12, 14, 26, 198
terminology, 35–42
training process, 7–9
See also Aids; Balance; Ground work; Rules; Saddle work; Work in hand
Transitions, 191–196, *192*
Trotting, 168, 188, 193
True balance, 93–97, *94–95, 97*
Turning, 122–123, *123–125*
Turn on the forehand, 199

Walk and halt-halts, 187
Whips, 118, 127, 130, 154
Working gaits, 89–92, *90*
Work in hand, 129–159
allowed stop, 126, 132, *137*, 139
back relaxing, 37, 131
exercise-reward, 130, 151–152
falling out, 145
instructions, 131
muscle knots, 139, *141*, 141–142, *143*
Natural Circle, 147–150, *149, 151*
nosebands for, 130
over bending, 139, *140*
rein holding, *144*, 145
shoulders/quarters, 145–147, *146, 148*
softening body, 142, *144*, 144–145
softening jaw/poll, 131–132, *133–136*
staying soft, *138*, 139
tack for, 130
whip aid, 130
See also Ground work; Longeing; Rein aids

Xenophon, 15